Grammar in Context

Geoff Barton

OXFORD
UNIVERSITY PRESS

OXFORD
UNIVERSITY PRESS

Great Clarendon Street, Oxford OX2 6DP

Oxford University Press is a department of the University of Oxford.
It furthers the University's objective of excellence in research, scholarship,
and education by publishing worldwide in

Oxford New York

Athens Auckland Bangkok Bogotá Buenos Aires Calcutta
Cape Town Chennai Dar es Salaam Delhi Florence Hong Kong Istanbul
Karachi Kuala Lumpur Madrid Melbourne Mexico City Mumbai
Nairobi Paris São Paulo Singapore Taipei Tokyo Toronto Warsaw

with associated companies in Berlin Ibadan

Oxford is a registered trade mark of Oxford University Press
in the UK and in certain other countries

First published 1999
Reprinted 1999

Printed in Italy

ISBN 0 19 831450 7

Contents

Introduction

Grammar in Context

Grammar in Context joins *Comprehension to 14* and *Grammar to 14* as a further step in teaching students the essential skills they will need to succeed in English. The series has shown that basic skills don't have to be dull, arid and worthy. Both *Comprehension to 14* and *Grammar to 14* pay close attention to developing specific skills in writing, reading, understanding, and response, while keeping activities and stimulus materials lively and interesting.

This book takes all of that a stage further, showing students how close grammatical attention to texts can help them understand texts better, write more effectively – and boost their grades in English.

This is the part of English work that many students find the most tricky. We can teach them about grammar and develop their grammatical understanding through exercises and drills. But how do students then transfer that understanding into reflecting on their own work or responding more accurately to the texts they read?

Grammar in Context is the logical next step. It shows students how an understanding of grammatical principles can be applied to a variety of texts, making their response more systematic and thoughtful. And it shows them how to apply their grammatical knowledge to their reading and writing.

Key features

A reassuring Q & A section for students

We all learn most effectively when we know *why* we're learning something. This section shows students how greater understanding of grammar can have a real impact on their reading and writing. It is the essential starting-point for students to take control of their own learning.

Section 1: Grammar foundations

Increasingly, all forms of testing in English require an explicit knowledge of grammar. Students without that knowledge find themselves at a considerable disadvantage. The question for teachers is: how much grammar do students need to know?

In the past, grammar has been rooted too much at word level; testing grammar involved getting students to quack the various parts of speech. This is fine if there is no greater purpose in knowing about grammar.

Fortunately, that limited view of grammar has now been replaced by a broader and more practical definition. Section 1 of *Grammar in Context* emphasizes the sentence and discourse levels of grammar – looking at how writers organize their texts structurally and in sentences – before moving systematically through the other layers of grammatical knowledge. This is a more rewarding approach for students because they begin to develop an understanding of the way writers' linguistic decisions – such as choice of sentence types – have a real impact on the effect of their texts.

Grammar in itself will not teach students how to be better readers. Crucially, they need to know how to apply their grammatical knowledge to texts. The Grammar Foundations section therefore features a number of annotated texts, showing students what kind of points they might make when responding to the language of a passage.

Section 2: Grammar in context

Once students are secure in the fundamentals of grammar they can begin to examine in more detail how grammar is used to create texts.

Section 2 is organized by genre, and includes a range of fiction, non-fiction and media texts. Each genre is introduced by a sample text, showing students some of the grammatical and stylistic features associated with that genre, and illustrating the kinds of points they might make when writing about texts. The suggestion here is that students look at the genre samples whilst covering up the language comments which follow the extract. They could discuss or make notes on their ideas, before reading the notes provided. This offers students an active model for analysing texts, based on small samples.

Students then encounter longer passages accompanied by questions which have been devised to develop their understanding of the effect grammatical and lexical decisions can have on a text.

Writing assignments at the end of each unit encourage students to experiment with grammatical structures and devices, and analyse the effects.

This is not, therefore, just another comprehension book. A systematic approach to working with the text in class will teach students to become more analytical readers – the kind of readers who spot the details in texts and do well in exams.

Section 3: Your writing

A final section of more extended writing activities offers a chance for summative assessment: students can demonstrate what they have learnt as they tackle assignments on the writing of narratives, letters, reports and leaflets.

Answer Book

To support all of this we have written an Answer Book. This gives students photocopiable answer sheets, plus sample answers. Students can learn a lot about how to improve their own answers by looking at and reflecting on other examples – something which is not always easy to manage amid the day-to-day demands of classroom life. This book provides you with the resources you'll need. We have also included materials to support less able students, to build their grammatical knowledge and show them how they can, with practice, make real progress in answering the questions.

Conclusion

We all know that our most successful students respond not just to the content of texts, but to the nuances of language. I imagine we all wish that more of our students had similar analytical skills. *Grammar in Context* is written to develop exactly those skills in students who might otherwise respond at a more general level of personal response unsupported by analysis. The book is designed to increase their knowledge, confidence and – unashamedly – their English marks.

I hope you'll find it an asset in your classroom.

Geoff Barton

Section 1

Grammar foundations

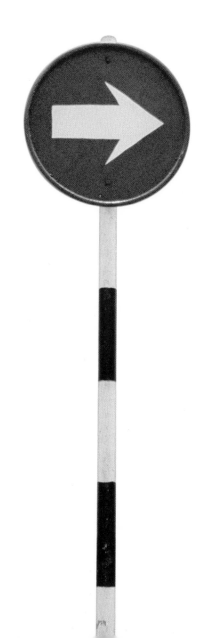

Student Q & A

What's grammar?

Grammar is the way we organize language – putting words, phrases and sentences into an order that makes sense to our audience.

Almost as soon as we are born, we begin to learn that words have to go together in a certain order to make sense.

The cat on the sick is carpet has been

doesn't make sense. It is **un**grammatical.

The cat has been sick on the carpet

does make sense. It is grammatical.

From around the age of one, children begin putting words together to say what they mean – for example:

my cat   *big dog*

It would be unusual for a child to say:

cat my

The child has begun to learn about grammar patterns – that words can't just go in any order.

(The child might learn that you could say:

dog big

Think of a situation where a child might say this. How is 'dog big' different in meaning from 'big dog'?)

Why do I need to know about grammar?

You already do know a lot about it: from around five years old you've been using it highly effectively. But if you want to do well in English you need to know how to apply that grammatical knowledge.

What do you mean, 'apply'?

Put it this way: the best students at 14, 16 and 18 tend to do more than read and write well. They read texts analytically, responding not just to the ideas in them, but also to the style. Their own written style tends to be lively, interesting and accurate. You can only really achieve that if you learn how to make specific grammar points based on your reading, and use a variety of styles in your writing.

So knowing about grammar will improve my English marks?

Knowing about how language works can help you to be a better reader. It enables you to say in more detail how a text has been put together by the writer. Being able to write a grammatical sentence will help you to make your meaning understood by your reader, but, beyond that, knowing about grammar will also improve your written style.

So how will this book help me?

Grammar in Context starts by showing you the essential grammar knowledge you'll need to use in English. Then it shows you how to apply this to a range of different texts. Then it gives you practice. The Answer Book even provides sample answers so that you can compare your own work with them to see how you're doing.

The result?

You should end up a better reader and writer in English because you'll be more aware of the essential skills that are required.

What grammar skills will I need?

You will need to be able to look at a text and make some detailed comments about how it works. This might mean:

- commenting on the structure of paragraphs and ideas
- commenting on the sentence structures
- commenting on the writer's choice of words.

This Grammar Foundations section will quickly teach you the essential grammar information you need. It will then show you how to apply it to your reading.

To understand grammar, you need to know that there are different levels of language use:

Whole text level
This is the way texts are organized into sections or paragraphs; the way paragraphs themselves are structured; the way openings and closings in different kinds of texts work. It is sometimes called *discourse structure*.

Sentence level
This involves looking at sentences, clauses and phrases; the way units of meaning are linked together with words like *although* or *and*; the use of main clauses (giving the main information in a sentence) and subordinate clauses (giving background information).

Word level
This involves looking at the specific words a writer has chosen; how the words are structured; what function they have in the sentence.

Punctuation
Running through all of this is punctuation. Punctuation is the way the writer shows a reader where different units of meaning start and end (capital letters and full stops), or where someone is speaking (direct speech or speech marks), and so on.

This section will teach you what you need to know about these different levels of grammar.

And if I need more help?

Look at our website and email me for any advice. I'll do my best to respond to you personally with answers to your questions.

Website: http://www.oup.co.uk/exam.success

Email: geoff.barton@oup.co.uk

Good luck with your English studies.

Geoff Barton

What you need to know about...

Whole texts

Key facts   ### Text-level grammar

> When you're looking at 'the grammar of whole texts', you're looking at the way texts are organized. That might include:
> - use of layout
> - openings and closings
> - paragraphs

Look at the newspaper story below. It is about the language some teenagers use in informal situations – language that is called slang.

As you read the article, look at the margin notes. These show you some of the main features of the text.

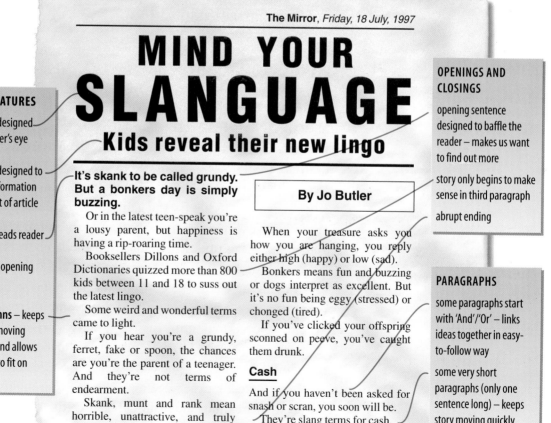

LAYOUT FEATURES

headline – designed to catch reader's eye

strapline – designed to give more information about subject of article

bold text – leads reader into story by emphasizing opening sentence

text in columns – keeps reader's eye moving down page, and allows more stories to fit on page

OPENINGS AND CLOSINGS

opening sentence designed to baffle the reader – makes us want to find out more

story only begins to make sense in third paragraph

abrupt ending

PARAGRAPHS

some paragraphs start with 'And'/'Or' – links ideas together in easy-to-follow way

some very short paragraphs (only one sentence long) – keeps story moving quickly

---

The Mirror, Friday, 18 July, 1997

MIND YOUR SLANGUAGE
Kids reveal their new lingo

It's skank to be called grundy. But a bonkers day is simply buzzing.

Or in the latest teen-speak you're a lousy parent, but happiness is having a rip-roaring time.

Booksellers Dillons and Oxford Dictionaries quizzed more than 800 kids between 11 and 18 to suss out the latest lingo.

Some weird and wonderful terms came to light.

If you hear you're a grundy, ferret, fake or spoon, the chances are you're the parent of a teenager. And they're not terms of endearment.

Skank, munt and rank mean horrible, unattractive, and truly awful.

By Jo Butler

When your treasure asks you how you are hanging, you reply either high (happy) or low (sad).

Bonkers means fun and buzzing or dogs interpret as excellent. But it's no fun being eggy (stressed) or chonged (tired).

If you've clicked your offspring sconned on peeve, you've caught them drunk.

Cash

And if you haven't been asked for snash or scran, you soon will be.

They're slang terms for cash.

Practice   Now look at the next piece of text, at the foot of the page.

What do you notice about:

- the layout
- openings and closings
- paragraphs?

Hints   *Layout*
Look at the title.
Look at the way the ingredients are listed.
Look at the way the instructions are set out in three paragraphs.

Openings and closings
Look at the first paragraph and notice how it is different from the other two – it doesn't really give instructions.
Look at the ending – does it end at a logical point, or does it feel abrupt?

Paragraphs
Notice that paragraphs seem quite short – why do you think this is?
Look at the way one paragraph links with another – for example the word 'Now' in paragraph 3.

The 30-minute Cook

A Quick Lamb Curry
. . . .

For 2

-
25g/1oz butter

1 tablespoon groundnut oil

450g/1lb cubed lamb

1 medium onion, chopped

3 cloves of garlic, crushed

1 cinnamon stick, broken in two

6 green cardamom pods, crushed open

1 teaspoon ground cumin

1 teaspoon ground ginger

1 tablespoon garam masala

1 teaspoon chilli powder

A dry curry, delectably spicy and aromatic rather than blisteringly hot. To be scooped from your plate with any of the Indian breads on sale at the supermarket, warm from the grill or oven.

Melt the butter in a deep-sided frying-pan and add the oil; when it starts to sizzle fry the lamb till just coloured on each side. Remove with a draining spoon. Add the onion and fry till golden, scraping up any residue from the lamb at the same time. Add the garlic and fry for a minute more.

Now add the whole spices. Cook for 2 minutes or until the cardamom pods have coloured a little and then add the ground spices. Cook until their fragrance starts to rise, but make sure they do not burn. Return the lamb to the pan. Pour in 225ml/8fl oz water – you can use meat or vegetable stock if you have some knocking around – and stir thoroughly. Turn the heat to medium and simmer gently till the sauce has thickened, about 10–15 minutes.

What you need to know about...

Sentences 1: sentence lengths

Key facts   Sentences

A **sentence** is a unit of meaning which can stand on its own and make sense. Almost all writing is structured in sentences.

'Now add the whole spices' is a sentence.

'Now add' is not a sentence (because we're not told what to add).

'The whole spices' is not a sentence (because we aren't told what to do with the spices).

Key facts   Sentence lengths

Sentences can be different lengths, creating different effects.

Short sentences can help to build suspense:

The night was dark. The moon was hidden. The footsteps crunched on the drive.

Longer sentences can help to explain complicated ideas:

Jon Wolfert, the most successful producer of radio jingles in the USA, started with a love of radio and has never looked back, despite all the competition.

Practice One comment you can often make about a text is the length of sentences.

Look again at this extract from the recipe for lamb curry. The margin notes show you the kinds of points you could make about the length of the sentences.

longer sentence containing three instructions – parts of sentence linked by 'or' and 'and'

short sentence – helps make it clear what you have to do

Now add the whole spices. Cook for 2 minutes or until the cardamom pods have coloured a little and then add the ground spices. Cook until their fragrance starts to rise, but make sure they do not burn. Return the lamb to the pan.

quite lengthy sentence containing two main ideas

short final sentence – sums up what you need to do

Writing about sentence length can be quite useful, but for higher marks there are other points you need to learn to make – about the different types of sentences and how they work.

There are **simple sentences**, **compound sentences**, and **complex sentences**. All three types of sentences are made up of **clauses**.

What you need to know about...

Sentences 2: sentence types

Key facts   Clauses

> A **clause** is a group of words built around a verb.
> We place them together to form sentences.

Key facts   Simple sentences

> A **simple sentence** communicates one idea.
> One thing (usually) happens in a simple sentence.
>
> *The night was dark.*
> *Now add the spices.*
>
> A simple sentence is made up of one clause.

Simple sentences can be very dramatic, so they are ideal for creating suspense. They are also very clear so they are often used for giving instructions. In addition, they feel safe, simple, reassuring and straightforward. That's one reason you find them so often in children's books.

Key facts   Compound sentences

> **Compound sentences** communicate more than one idea.
> A compound sentence consists of two or more simple sentences which are linked by the words *and*, *or*, or *but*.

This compound sentence contains two clauses:

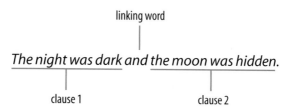

linking word

The night was dark and the moon was hidden.

clause 1   clause 2

This compound sentence contains three clauses:

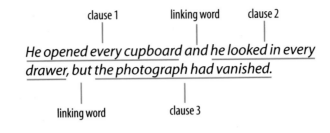

He opened every cupboard and he looked in every drawer, but the photograph had vanished.

clause 1   linking word   clause 2

linking word   clause 3

Key facts

Complex sentences

Complex sentences also communicate more than one idea. A complex sentence consists of several clauses. At least one of them will be the **main clause**, which carries the main meaning of the sentence. But there will also be one or more **subordinate clauses**, which give more information about what is happening, e.g.:

subordinate clause

As soon as Mel entered the room, she recognized the girl.

main clause

The subordinate clause is the clause which adds another action to the sentence, but which could not make sense on its own.

Subordinate clauses often begin with the following words:

who	since	that
whom	until	in case
whose	before	so
which	because	if
that	how	unless
when	than	though
where	as much as	although
as	so that	even though

Practice

Look at the following examples of complex sentences. See if you can pick out which part is the main clause and which is the subordinate clause.

Our hamster, which had been my pet for two years, got out of his cage.
We sat for ages in the car which was getting hotter and hotter.

The man who lives next door started shouting.

The goldfish which had been swimming around all day suddenly stopped moving.

I didn't finish the book, although I liked the storyline.

After I had finished my tea, I went outside.

However hard I try, I just don't understand this work.

Because he was in a bad mood, I just ignored him.

Looking at clauses in texts

It's useful to be able to spot the different types of sentences on their own. But you also need to be able to say something about how they work in longer texts.

Look again at the extract from the recipe for lamb curry. Look at the kinds of points you might make about the sentence and clause structure:

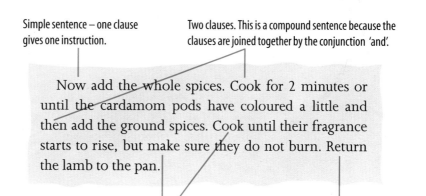

Simple sentence – one clause gives one instruction.

Two clauses. This is a compound sentence because the clauses are joined together by the conjunction 'and'.

> Now add the whole spices. Cook for 2 minutes or until the cardamom pods have coloured a little and then add the ground spices. Cook until their fragrance starts to rise, but make sure they do not burn. Return the lamb to the pan.

A two-clause sentence. It is a compound sentence because the two clauses are linked by the conjunction 'but'.

Simple sentence

In an exam or test, it is useful to be able to spot language features like this, but for higher marks you need to be able to comment more on the *effect* of the sentence structure.

A good answer might say:

> The pattern of the sentences in the text is a mixture of simple and compound sentences. The conjunctions <u>and</u> and <u>but</u> are used to link clauses together and this keeps the text moving, stopping it becoming too abrupt and disjointed. The final simple sentence keeps the instructions very clear.

What you need to know about...

Phrases

Key facts   Phrases

> **Phrases** are groups of words which cannot usually stand alone. Here are some examples:
>
> *the large ice cream*
> *on the bus*
> *sitting alone*
> *around the corner*

The most important phrase you need to know about is the noun phrase.

Key facts   The noun phrase

> A **noun phrase** is a group of words built around a naming word, or noun. Noun phrases allow writers to add detail to their nouns, like this:
>
> *the cat*
> *the old cat*
> *the old fat cat*
> *the old fat black cat*
>
> All of these are phrases, but each one has a greater level of detail, telling us more about the cat.

Knowing about phrases can be useful when writing about texts. They can help you to say how descriptive a text is. Look at this example, taken from Laurie Lee's account of his earliest memories:

The June grass, amongst which I stood, was taller than I was, and I wept. I had never been so close to grass before. It towered above me and all around me, each blade tattooed with tiger-skins of sunlight. It was knife-edged, dark, and a wicked green, thick as a forest and alive with grasshoppers that chirped and chattered and leapt through the air like monkeys.

I was lost and didn't know where to move. A tropic heat oozed up from the ground, rank with sharp odours of roots and nettles. Snow-clouds of elder-blossom banked in the sky, showering upon me the fumes and the flakes of their sweet and giddy suffocation. High overhead ran frenzied larks, screaming, as though the sky were tearing apart.

Here are some of the comments you could make about noun phrases in this extract.

'Tiger-skins of sunlight' – this phrase helps us to see exactly what the sunlight was like. It suggests a pattern of stripes – light then dark – perhaps in a strong orangey yellow colour.

'Tropic heat' – this phrase gives us a really powerful sense of the weather. 'Tropic' suggests extremely hot and sticky.

'Snow-clouds of elder blossom' – this phrase makes the blossom seem brilliant white and thick, like white clouds.

'Sweet and giddy suffocation' – suggests that the scent of the blossom is pleasant ('sweet') and makes him feel dizzy ('giddy'), and that it's quite overpowering ('suffocation').

'Frenzied larks' – suggests the mad, rapid movement of the birds.

As you can see, paying close attention to the writer's use of phrases allows you to comment in detail on the effect of the writing.

Watch out in newspaper articles for the way writers use phrases to label people:

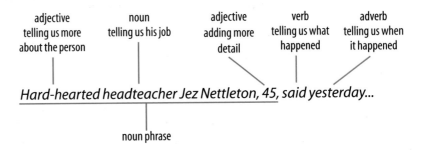

All of these parts of the phrase give more detail about the subject. They allow the writer to pile up the information without using clauses, which would create a much longer opening:

> *Jez Nettleton, who is 45 and who is a headteacher and who is hard-hearted said today, ...*

Why do you think it is especially important to journalists to keep their use of language compact, so that it takes up as little space as possible?

Key facts   **Phrases and participles**

Noun phrases tell us more about the noun in the sentence: they add description. But phrases can also give us more information about what is going on in a sentence. They do this by using a **participle**. The participle is the part of the verb that ends in '-ing':

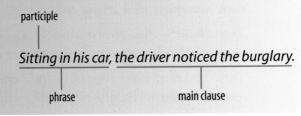

Like a subordinate clause, the participle gives us extra information:

> *Eating her dinner, Aunt Mary felt rather unwell.*
> *Hoping she was in time, the girl ran to school.*
> *The bus broke down, making us all late.*
> *The treehouse wobbled in the wind, looking fairly unsafe.*

What you need to know about...

Words 1: formal and informal words

Key facts   Simple and complex words

In an exam or test, there are all kinds of things you might say about the way words are used in texts.

You might say whether the words are **simple** or **complex**. This can have a big effect on what a text feels like – whether it is easy to follow, or complicated.

Simple words may be words we use everyday. They may have just one or two syllables. Complex words may be less familiar words, with more syllables, making them seem more formal.

Look at these examples of simple and complex words:

Simple	**Complex**
house	residence
food	sustenance
get round	outmanoeuvre

These words are simple because they are:
● familiar
● one syllable long.

These words are complex because they are:
● less familiar
● three or four syllables long.

Key facts   Word origins

Why are some words familiar and others not? One reason is that many of the words we use in everyday language are **Anglo-Saxon** words – they have been used in English for hundreds of years. We use them to describe the things around us in straightforward terms.

Other words are known as **loan words**. They are words that have passed into English from other languages, such as French, Latin or Greek. They are often used in more formal writing, rather than in everyday speech.

Practice

1 Look at these two lists of words. On the left are words of Anglo-Saxon origin. They are more straightforward words which we would expect to find in less formal texts. On the right are loan words with similar meanings, but which are more complex. We would expect to find them in more complex texts.

Try to match up words with similar meanings from the two lists. The first one is done for you as an example.

Informal (Anglo-Saxon)	**Formal (loan word)**
A find	**1** encounter
B kind	**2** bacteria
C early	**3** juvenile
D mad	**4** location
E germ	**5** premature
F young	**6** replenish
G place	**7** hospitable
H fill	**8** eccentric

2 Look at the two extracts of text below. Knowing about the complexity of words can help you to comment on the way the texts have been written.

These two texts are the openings of modern fairy tales. You might expect both to have simple vocabulary because they are written for children.

The Iron Man

The Iron Man came to the top of the cliff.

How far had he walked? Nobody knows. Where had he come from? Nobody knows.

Taller than a house, the Iron Man stood at the top of the cliff, on the very brink, in the darkness.

The wind sang through his iron fingers. His great iron head, shaped like a dustbin but as big as a bedroom, slowly turned to the right, slowly turned to the left. His iron ears turned, this way, that way. He was hearing the sea. His eyes, like headlamps, glowed white, then red, then infra-red, searching the sea. Never before had the Iron Man seen the sea.

Ted Hughes

🌸 The Good Little Girl 🌸

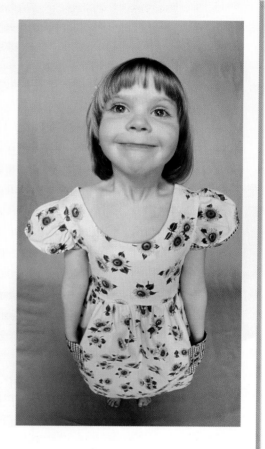

Her name was Priscilla Prodgers, and she was a very good little girl indeed. So good was she, in fact, that she could not help being aware of it herself, and that is a stage to which very many quite excellent persons never succeed in attaining. She was only just a child, it is true, but she had read a great many beautiful storybooks, and so she knew what a powerful reforming influence a childish and innocent remark, or a youthful example or a happy combination of both, can exert over grown-up people.

F Anstey

Although they are both fairy tales, these two texts feel very different. *The Iron Man* is simpler and more direct because:

The Iron Man came to the top of the cliff.

How far had he walked? Nobody knows. Where had he come from? Nobody knows.

Taller than a house, the Iron Man stood at the top of the cliff, on the very brink, in the darkness.

The wind sang through his iron fingers. His great iron head, shaped like a dustbin but as big as a bedroom, slowly turned to the right, slowly turned to the left. His iron ears turned, this way, that way. He was hearing the sea. His eyes, like headlamps, glowed white, then red, then infra-red, searching the sea. Never before had the Iron Man seen the sea.

SENTENCES

it uses shorter sentences

it uses simple sentences – sentences containing just one clause.

WORDS

it uses mostly words of one syllable

it uses familiar words

The Good Little Girl feels more complex because:

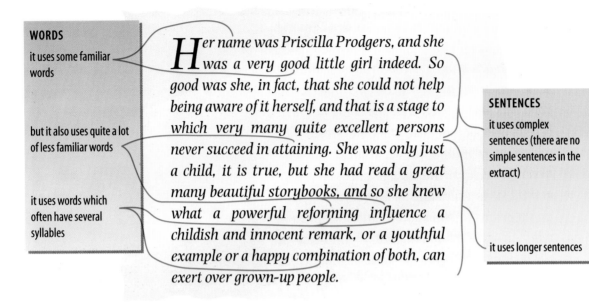

WORDS

it uses some familiar words

but it also uses quite a lot of less familiar words

it uses words which often have several syllables

Her name was Priscilla Prodgers, and she was a very good little girl indeed. So good was she, in fact, that she could not help being aware of it herself, and that is a stage to which very many quite excellent persons never succeed in attaining. She was only just a child, it is true, but she had read a great many beautiful storybooks, and so she knew what a powerful reforming influence a childish and innocent remark, or a youthful example or a happy combination of both, can exert over grown-up people.

SENTENCES

it uses complex sentences (there are no simple sentences in the extract)

it uses longer sentences

The overall effect is NOT that one text is better than the other. Instead, it's that one is more direct and straightforward; the other is more complex.

What you need to know about...

Words 2: word classes

Key facts   Word classes

> **Word classes** are the names we give to the *functions* of words in sentences – what the words do.

For example:

The	*girl*	*swam*	*in*	*the*	*river*

Look at the word *swam*. It tells us what the girl was doing. It comes from the word class 'verbs'. We could change it to all kinds of other words which serve the same function (i.e. other verbs):

The	*girl*	*swam*	*in*	*the*	*river*
		fell			
		jumped			
		sang			
		laughed			

But there are lots of words that wouldn't work:

The	*girl*	*swam*	*in*	*the*	*river*
		the			
		table			
		if			

The, *table*, and *if* don't work because they are not from the word class 'verbs'. They come from different word classes, which do different things within a sentence.

This is what a word class is – a category of words which have a particular function in a sentence.

Checklist of word classes

Word Class	Explanation	Examples	Notes
Verbs	tell us what happened – what someone or something actually did	eat, think, go, do	Verbs have tenses to tell us when things happened – past, present and future: I ate my breakfast/ I was eating my breakfast I eat my breakfast/I am eating my breakfast I will eat my breakfast / I am going to eat my breakfast Verbs that tell you about the tense are called auxiliary verbs: *was* eating, *have* eaten, *will be* eating
Adverbs	add detail to the verb – telling us how something happened	swam *slowly*, swam *happily*, swam *fast*	Other adverbs tell us about time – yesterday, now, then
Nouns	the names of things, people and places	clock, cat, Glasgow, Postman Pat	Concrete nouns are things we can touch (clock, river, hat) Abstract nouns are ideas (hope, happiness, death)
Adjectives	Add detail to nouns	the *large* clock, the *ticking* clock, the *broken* clock, the *blue* clock	Adjectives usually come in front of the noun – they are sometimes referred to as 'describing words'
Prepositions	Tell us where something is	on, under, through, behind, inside	We sometimes use prepositions with verbs, giving them a more informal feel: get *on* think *about* talk *through*

Word Class	Explanation	Examples	Notes
Pronouns	stand in place of a noun to avoid repetition, and help the reader foliow what is going on	When the man saw the accident, *he* called the police he, she, they, we, us, them	Without 'he' you would have to repeat 'the man'
Conjunctions	join words, phrases, clauses and sentences together	I like the cat *and* the cat likes me.	The most common conjunctions are: *and, or, but.* Others include: *if, although, because, however*

What you need to know about...

Words 3: word structure

Key facts **Units of meaning**

Many words can be broken down into smaller **units of meaning**. These are not the same as syllables: *e-le-phant* is a three-syllable word, but it does not have three different units of meaning. *Un+happi+ness* does contain three units of meaning.

The key ingredients of words are the **base form** (or **root**), **prefixes**, **suffixes**, and **inflections**.

Key facts **The base form**

The **base form** is the core of a word, the part that cannot be divided into smaller units of meaning – for example:

wise   dog   cycle

Key facts **Prefixes**

Prefixes are elements we add to the *front* of the base form to change its meaning:

un+wise   under+dog   bi+cycle

Prefixes can change the meaning of words in several ways. Some say 'not':

un+wise   dis+obey   non-smoker

Some say something about size:

market – super+market

Others tell you where something happens:

way – sub+way

...Or add information about numbers:

cycle – bi+cycle

Key facts   **Suffixes**

Elements added to the *ends* of words are **suffixes**.

Some change verbs into nouns:

amuse+ment
fight+er

...Or adjectives into verbs:

modern+ize
simple+ify

...Or nouns into adjectives:

hero+ic
child+ish

Some make a word more abstract:

spoon+ful
race+ism

Notice that some base words lose a letter or change their spelling when they gain a suffix:

race+ism = racism
happy+ness = happiness

Key facts   **Inflections**

One important group of suffixes is used to tell us

● how many nouns there are
● the tense of a verb.

These are called **inflections**. Adding one of these suffixes is often called 'inflecting a noun' or 'inflecting a verb'.

Inflecting a noun to make a plural (more than one):

cat+s
child+ren

Inflecting a verb to change tense:

throw+ing　　　*throw+s*

Inflecting adjectives and adverbs:

hot – hotter – hottest

Practice

1　Add different prefixes to each of these words, and describe how the meaning of the word changes. The first one is done for you.

Prefix	Base word	Change of meaning
un	1 cover 2 view 3 appear 4 water 5 ground 6 heated	makes it mean the opposite

2　Add suffixes to these words and describe how their meaning changes.

Base word	Suffix	Change of meaning
hope kind king lion station		

3　Inflect these words to change their meaning, using the instruction to guide you:

Base word	Inflection	Change of meaning
clean		change to past tense
car		change to plural form
small		change to the 'most small'

Section 2

Grammar in context

Fiction

Fiction is imaginary writing – in other words, stories. There are dozens of different fiction genres, such as fairytales, crime fiction, romance, science fiction, ghost stories. All of them aim to draw the reader into a world which the writer creates through language. Some fiction genres emphasize plot (for example, legends and thrillers); some emphasize description (for example, Thomas Hardy's novels of the late nineteenth century); some use dialogue to show us the thoughts and feelings of characters; some use first person mode to tell us the story through the main character's eyes ('I...' rather than 'she...').This section shows you how close attention to the language used by fiction writers can help you to understand their texts better.

Genre sample

The sample text below is followed by some suggestions of the kinds of grammar and vocabulary points you might make. To start, you might cover the comments section, read the text, and think what you would say about its tone, vocabulary, and structure, and about the type of sentences the writer has used.

In the kitchen of a small farm a little woman sat cutting bread and butter. The glow of the clear, ruddy fire was on her shining cheek and white apron; but grey hair will not take the warm caress of firelight.

She skilfully spread the softened butter, and cut off great slices from the floury loaf in her lap. Already two plates were piled, but she continued to cut.

Outside the naked ropes of the creeper tapped and lashed at the window.

D H Lawrence, *A Prelude*

Comments

What could you say about tone?

The writer uses a detached, descriptive tone. Using a third person narrative ('She skilfully') rather than first person mode ('I skilfully') keeps us distant from the woman's feelings: we cannot yet tell what she is thinking. The writer tells us a little about the woman and her house, but keeps us wondering. We are not sure who she is, where she is, or what is going to happen. This hooks our interest and makes us want to read on.

What could you say about vocabulary?

The writer writes precisely, using vocabulary which helps us to visualize the scene. He uses adjectives to give detail to nouns: *small* farm; *clear, ruddy* fire; *shining* cheek; *white* apron. These help to make the scene more specific.

What could you say about sentences?

The writer uses a variety of sentence types – simple and complex – and these add to the interest of the extract. They help to keep us reading.

What could you say about structure?

The first two paragraphs focus on the woman. The pronoun *she* shows that the woman remains the central subject. Then paragraph three surprises us: the focus changes to the creeper outside. It makes us wonder what is going on, and creates a feeling of tension.

Review

The writer uses a typical fictional technique – holding back information to make the reader want to read on. The technique is used most in ghost stories and crime fiction. It has the effect of driving us forward into the text. A newspaper story would take a different approach: it would aim to tell us the whole story as quickly as possible. In fiction, however, the writer can afford to control the pace, and hold the reader's interest through tension.

Going further

We are now going to look at how writers use different styles of language to tell stories.

This is the opening of a short story from Scotland. It is a good example of how a writer can use dialogue to move the story on and to reveal his characters. Read the passage and then answer the questions which follow.

Neil M. Gunn

The Tax-Gatherer

'Blast it,' he muttered angrily. 'Where is the accursed place?'

He looked at the map again spread before him on the steering-wheel. Yes, it should be just here. There was the cross-roads. He threw a glance round the glass of his small saloon car and saw a man's head bobbing beyond the hedge. At once he got out and walked along the side of the road.

'Excuse me,' he cried. The face looked at him over the hedge. 'Excuse me, but can you tell me where Mrs Martha Williamson stays?'

'Mrs Who?'

'Mrs Martha Williamson.'

'No,' said the face slowly, and moved away. He followed it for a few paces to a gap in the hedge. 'No,' said the man again, and turned to call a spaniel out of the turnips. He had a gun under his arm and was obviously a gamekeeper.

'Well, she lives about here, at Ivy Cottage.'

'Ivy Cottage? Do you mean the tinkers?' And the gamekeeper regarded him thoughtfully.

'Yes. I suppose so.'

'I see,' said the gamekeeper, looking away. 'Turn up to your right at the cross-roads there and you'll see it standing back from the road.'

He thanked the gamekeeper and set off, walking quickly so that he needn't think too much about his task, for it was new to him.

When he saw the cottage, over amongst some bushes with a rank growth of nettles at one end, he thought it a miserable place, but when he came close to the peeling limewash, the torn-down ivy, the sagging roof, the broken stone doorstep thick with trampled mud, he saw that it was a wretched hovel.

The door stood half-open, stuck. He knocked on it and listened to the acute silence. He knocked again firmly and thought he heard thin whisperings. He did not like the hushed fear in the sounds, and was just about to knock peremptorily when there was a shuffling, and, quietly as an apparition, a woman was there.

She stood twisted, lax, a slim, rather tall figure, with a face the colour of the old limewash. She clung to the edge of the door in a manner unhumanly pathetic, and looked at him out of dark, soft eyes.

'Are you Mrs Williamson?'

After a moment she said, 'Yes.'

'Well, I've come about that dog. Have you taken out the licence yet?'

'No.'

'Well, it's like this,' he said, glancing away from her. 'We don't want to get you into trouble. But the police reported to us that you had the dog. Now, you can't have a dog without paying a licence. You know that. So, in all the circumstances, the authorities decided that if you paid a compromise fine of seven-and-six, and took out the licence, no more would be said about it. You would not be taken to court.' He looked at her again, and saw no less than five small heads poking round her ragged dark skirt. 'We don't want you to get into trouble,' he said. 'But you've got to pay by Friday – or you'll be summonsed. There's no way out.'

She did not speak, stood there unmoving, clinging to the door, a feminine creature waiting dumbly for the blow.

'Have you a husband?' he asked.

'Yes,' she said, after a moment.

'Where is he?'

'I don't know,' she answered, in her soft, hopeless voice. He wanted to ask her if he had left her for good, but could not, and this irritated him, so he said calmly, 'Well, that's the position, as you know. I was passing, and, seeing we had got no word of your payment, I thought I'd drop in and warn you. We don't want to take you to court. So my advice to you is to pay up – and at once, or it will be too late.'

Task B

Based on your reading of *The Tax-Gatherer*, explore further how dialogue can be used to tell stories. Imagine this scene: two complete strangers are travelling in silence in a lift in a large store. One of the two people suffers from claustrophobia (fear of confined spaces). Suddenly the lights flicker and the lift shudders to a halt.

Create the opening of a story using dialogue.
You should:

- choose words which will reveal what the characters are like

- use language structures which sound like spoken rather than written English

- decide how the characters should speak (e.g. nervously, cheerfully). Make sure their dialogue reveals how they feel.

- give variety to your text using different verbs, such as *spoke, uttered, snapped, whispered, muttered*, and so on.

Aim to write 500 words or so.

Fiction – focus on pre-1900 writing

The next extract, from Charles Dickens' novel *Great Expectations*, is an example of pre-1900 writing. The hero, Pip, is visiting the mysterious Miss Havisham. Miss Havisham is bored, and so has ordered Pip to entertain her by playing cards with her ward Estella. While they are playing, Pip begins to realize there is something very odd about Miss Havisham...

Charles Dickens   *Great Expectations*

*I*T WAS THEN I BEGAN TO UNDERSTAND that everything in the room had stopped, like the watch and the clock, a long time ago. I noticed that Miss Havisham put down the jewel exactly on the spot from which she had taken it up. As Estella dealt the cards, I glanced at the dressing-table again, and saw that the shoe upon it, once white, now yellow, had never been worn. I glanced down at the foot from which the shoe was absent, and saw that the silk stocking on it, once white, now yellow, had been trodden ragged. Without this arrest of everything, this standing still of all the pale decayed objects, not even the withered bridal dress on the collapsed form could have looked so like grave-clothes, or the long veil so like a shroud.

So she sat, corpse-like, as we played at cards; the frillings and trimmings on her bridal dress, looking like earthy paper. I knew nothing then of the discoveries that are occasionally made of bodies buried in ancient times, which fall to powder in the moment of being distinctly seen; but, I have often thought since, that she must have looked as if the admission of the natural light of day would have struck her to dust.

1 Pre-1900 writing often uses more complex structures and more formal vocabulary than present-day writing. Find three words or phrases which seem complex or formal.

2 The writer gives us the impression that Miss Havisham is almost like a person who has been dead for many years. He does this through the use of similes – where one object is compared with another. What similes does he use?

   a bridal dress compared with _____ (lines 8–10)

   b veil compared with _____ (lines 11–12)

   c frillings and trimmings compared with _____ (lines 15–17)

3 Write down two other examples of vocabulary the writer uses to create an impression of death in the room.

4 The passage is written in the first person: 'I noticed... I glanced...'. How would it feel different if it were written in the third person, without using *I* at all? (For instance, it might have begun, 'It was then he began to understand that everything in the room had stopped, like the watch and the clock, a long time ago. Miss Havisham put down...')

Advice   Does the first person style involve the reader more?
Make us understand Pip's feelings? Remind us that
we are reading someone's opinions rather than facts?

5 Do you think this passage is a good description of a mysterious character? Give reasons for your answer, looking particularly at:

   • the vocabulary Dickens used

   • the sentence structures.

Advice

Look at the way the words create an impression of decay. Look at the use of concrete nouns (*dressing-table*, *bridal dress*) to make the scene visual – as if we are actually in the room seeing these things.

Notice the complex sentences, full of details. How do these create an impression of a room which is full of objects and memories? How would the effect be different if the writer had used short sentences?

Writing

The text was written almost 150 years ago. How can you tell? How would you retell the story in a modern style for a modern audience? What changes would you make to the sentence structure? How would you change the vocabulary? Which details would you alter?

Rewrite the extract. Leave some parts the same, cut words, change the structure. Play around with the existing style to create a new style. Then write a one-paragraph commentary describing the changes you have made and how successful you think your new version of the text is.

Fiction – using powerful vocabulary

At the start of a story, writers often try to build up atmosphere by using powerful words. Read this opening from a thriller and then answer the questions which follow.

Edward Richard Rosset

Hot South Wind

'Thomas, are you going to eat your supper?'

The old woman eyed her son, a worried expression on her wrinkled face.

Outside, the gusty wind raised blinding dust in the deserted alleys of the little Spanish village.

Thomas grabbed the bottle of wine and had a long pull at it. 'I'm not hungry tonight, mother.' He wiped his mouth with his sleeve. 'I'll go to my room and lie down...'

Thomas's mother raised dark apprehensive eyes from her garlic soup. 'It's this cursed wind. I know it. Every time the wind blows hot something evil happens here. Remember last year when Pepe was found dead...'

Thomas spat into the fire. 'Bah, they all slipped on the ice down the Devil's Gorge, that's all...'

'And the year before, Maria was found stabbed to death in her bed...'

He shrugged his shoulders. 'A tramp was caught by the Guardia Civil later.'

A sudden strong gust made the old house tremble. The doors and windows moaned and creaked.

The frightened woman crossed herself quickly. 'Something is going to happen tonight,' she whispered, 'I can feel it. It's in the air...'

She was quite right. Something sinister was going to happen. Something as sinister as the death of the town mayor.

Thomas stretched himself noisily. 'I think I'll go to my room,' he said to his mother.

The lone yellowish electric bulb in the landing upstairs cast a grotesque wobbling shadow against the decaying smoky walls as he climbed the creaky stairs.

Outside the unpaved village streets were deserted.

Thomas checked his old pocket watch. Nine o'clock. Rodriguez shouldn't be long now. Every night Carmen's husband passed in front of the balcony to see his sheep before retiring.

Thomas remembered Carmen's long dark raven hair brushing her slender tanned shoulders. He saw in his mind once again the undulating soft movements of her hips, as she swayed along the path.

As he noiselessly slid open the balcony windows he shivered in the cold air.

He took a broken tile from the outjutting roof and careful weighed it in his hand. Tiles fall on windy days, don't they...?

Thomas was quite confident that he wouldn't miss. He had always been considered the best stone thrower in the whole valley.

Suddenly, there was a shadow moving towards his house. A faint pale beam peeping timidly from behind a dark grey threatening cloud glittered for a moment on Rodriguez's bald head.

This is the opening of a folk-tale from East Anglia. Read the passage and then answer the questions which follow.

❧ MOSSYCOAT ❧

THERE WAS ONCE A POOR old widow who lived in a little cottage. She had one daughter who was nineteen and very beautiful. Day after day her mother busied herself spinning a coat for her.

A pedlar came courting this girl. He called at the cottage regularly, and kept bringing her this trinket and that trinket. He was in love with her, and badly wanted her to marry him.

But the girl wasn't in love with him; things didn't work out as easily as that. She didn't know quite what to do for the best, and asked her mother for advice.

'Let him come,' said her mother. 'Get what you can out of him while I finish this coat. After that, you won't need him or his pretty little presents. You tell him, girl,' the mother said, 'that you won't marry him unless he gets you a white satin dress embroidered with sprigs of gold as big as a man's hand; and mind you tell him it must be a perfect fit.'

Next time the pedlar came round, and asked the daughter to marry him, she told him just this – the very same words her mother had used.

The pedlar looked at the girl, and took stock of her size and build. And within a week, he was back with the dress. It was made of white satin and embroidered with sprigs of gold, and when the girl went upstairs with her mother and tried it on, it was a perfect fit.

'What shall I do now, mother?' asked the girl.

'Tell him,' said the mother, 'that you won't marry him unless he gets you a dress made of silk the colour of all the birds of the air. And it must be a perfect fit.'

The girl told the pedlar just this, and in two or three days he was back at the cottage with the coloured silk dress. And since he knew her size from the first dress, of course it was a perfect fit.

'Now what shall I do?' asked the girl.

'Tell him,' said her mother, 'that you won't marry him unless he gets you a pair of silver slippers that are a perfect fit.'

The girl told the pedlar just this, and in a few days he called round with them. The girl's feet were only about three inches long, but the slippers were a perfect fit. They were not too tight; neither were they too loose.

1 **a** Write down two adjectives that the writer uses in the first sentence to describe the woman.

 b Now write down two adjectives with similar meanings which the writer might have used in the same places.

2 In the second paragraph the writer refers to 'this girl'. Why do you think he uses the word *this* rather than *the*? What effect does it have?

3 Like many folk tales, this one uses quite simple language. Find an example of a familiar word in each of these categories:

Noun
Verb
Adjective
Adverb

4 Look again at the first paragraph of the story. In what ways does it seem typical of the style of folk-tales or legends?

Advice   You could look at
• the opening words
• when the story is set
• the characters the story involves and the way they are described: do we learn a lot about their personalities? Do we identify with any of them? Whose viewpoint is the story told from?

5 Look again at the opening two sentences of the story. They both have a similar pattern: a main clause followed by a subordinate clause beginning with the word *who*.

Main clause	Subordinate clause
There was once a poor old woman	who lived in a cottage.
She had one daughter	who was nineteen and very beautiful.

How would the opening of the story be different if the writer had used four simple sentences instead? Rewrite the two sentences into four simple sentences by dropping the conjunction *who* and replacing it with *She* at the start of each new sentence.

Then try to explain, as precisely as you can, how the effect of the story has changed.

6 This extract can be divided into different stages. The writer has used discourse markers (words like *But, Next time*) and pronouns to link the different stages together.

   a See if you can divide the extract into stages – note down the words at the beginning and end of each stage.

   b Then try to pick out the words the writer has used to link each stage to the last or next one.

7 Compare the style of this extract with one of the other fiction extracts in this section. What are the similarities and what are the differences? Concentrate on how each extract is written: are the vocabulary and sentence structures simple or complex? Does the writer use a lot of adjectives, similes or figurative language, or is the style very simple? Write two short paragraphs on your findings.

Writing

How would the story be different if it were told in the present tense, as a spoken story rather than a written tale? Rewrite the first three paragraphs, telling the story in the present tense. Change other words that help you to tell the story better. Then write a sentence or two describing the effect. What changes have you made? How does the story feel different? In what ways is it an improvement on the original? Is it more effective, or less?

The first sentence is done for you.

There's a poor old widow who lives in a cottage...

Autobiography

Autobiography is personal writing – usually the story of the writer's own life.

Genre sample

In this sample text, Richard Rayner recalls his school days. To practise making more detailed comments about the language of autobiographical texts, read the extract, and think what you would say about it. Look in particular at the verbs the writer has chosen, at the use of pronouns, and at the sentence structures. Then look at the comments on the next page.

Stairs and corridors were covered with highly polished linoleum which squeaked as your sandals slid across it. You could hear someone coming fifty yards away. At the end of every corridor there was a tweed jacket, ready and waiting if you should dare to run. Running was forbidden, except on the playing fields, where we swarmed about in mud, beehives of boys pursuing one single soccer or rugby ball... It was the summer men walked on the moon. One Sunday my brother Keith, not my father, was waiting when I trooped out of chapel.

'Something's happened to Dad,' he said.

My father's clothes had been found on the beach at Deganwy. He was missing, presumed drowned.

Richard Rayner, *The Blue Suit*

Comments

What could you say about the whole text?
This is a memorable piece of autobiographical writing. The writer makes us picture the scene through lots of visual details. Then he hits us with a shock final sentence. The tone of the extract is quite unemotional, even at the end, when the writer is describing the disappearance of his father.

What could you say about sentences?
The sentences are mostly quite long. The writer uses relative clauses (e.g. 'linoleum *which squeaked*') to add detail to his main points, building a picture of life in the school. The last sentence is a short sentence. It contrasts with the earlier ones and gives the text real impact.

What could you say about verbs?
The writer has chosen visual verbs like *swarmed* and *trooped out* to help us to see the scene. *Swarmed* creates an impression of boys moving as a mass, like bees, while *trooped out* suggests the way the boys walked in a rough formation out of chapel.

What could you say about pronouns?
You helps the writer to involve the reader in the scene – it makes us imagine what it must have been like. *I* helps create a picture of the writer.

What could you say about the vocabulary?
Autobiography is always set in the past. Here, the writer uses details like the reference to the moon to tell the reader when the passage is set. He also uses nouns carefully and economically – for instance, he says, 'At the end of every corridor there was a tweed jacket waiting…', rather than 'a teacher in a tweed jacket.'

Going further

Now look at another extract from an autobiography: this time one which uses dialect words and simple vocabulary to tell the writer's story.

Autobiography – writing in the first person

Ronald Blythe looks back to his childhood in the Suffolk countryside and the people who played a part in his life.

Akenfield

Ronald Blythe

I was born during the bad times. My brothers and myself went to school for part of the day and to work for the rest of it. When we left school at half past three we'd go gleaning, picking up beans and all such things as that. We'd most likely work till eight if it stayed light. We biked to school at Framlingham. It was 1934 time. Things weren't very sharp. Father was making out by killing pigs for Danny Linton at Pettistree so we had to bike from school to home, eat some bread and cheese, or whatever there was – and there wasn't much – get an old sack and then bike on to Danny's farm to collect the pigs' insides. Then we biked home

with them and tipped them out on the scullery floor and scraped them. We had to get them as white as a board, scratching out all the filth with the back of an old knife. Then we washed them in salty water and – hey presto! – sausage skins. But it wasn't the end.

There were all these pails and pails of muck to be got rid of. We had to bike out of the village and bury it. On Saturdays we used to take a bundle

Akenfield   Ronald Blythe

of these skins to old Boot the butcher and he'd give us a three-cornered lump of brisket, all fat and bone, and weighing about a stone, in exchange. But even this is better than what happened in 1930, the big black year. In 1930 we had blackbird pie for Christmas dinner – and we had to catch the blackbirds before we had the pie! It had got to Christmas morning and we were going to make do when my father said, 'Come on, boys, let's try a blackbird!' We knocked a few over quite easy. I could take you to the spot where we did it. We cooked the pie in the brick oven.

This was the year my grandfather had to shut down the forge. He never went back to it. I used to walk by it, eyeing it and thinking. But nothing was rosy wherever you looked. Nearly everybody went out of business. Nothing was sold. People who had left school began to think about the Big House. You realized that it was there, with all the gardeners, grooms and maids and food. You have to face it, the Big House was then an asset to the village. It paid us to raise our hats, which is why we did it. I hear people run the gentry down now but they were better than the farmers in a crisis. Theirs was the only hand which fed us which we could see. So we bowed a bit; it cost nothing, even if it wasn't all courtesy. Nobody left, nobody went away. People were content. However hard up they were, they stayed content. The boys had the arse out of their trousers, no socks and the toes out of their boots. My brothers and myself were like this, yet so happy. I think other families were the same. The village kept close.

Word bank

gleaning	– sorting wheat from chaff
Framlingham	– town in mid-Suffolk
scullery	– utility room
brisket	– cheap cut of meat
forge	– blacksmith's workshop

1 The writer begins with a simple sentence. He might have started with a complex sentence like this: 'I was born during the bad times in which my brothers and myself went to school for part of the day and to work for the rest of it.' Why does the simple sentence make a more effective opening to the text?

2 Ronald Blythe uses straightforward vocabulary where some writers might have been tempted to choose more complex words.

   a For the verbs listed below, think of a more complex word with the same meaning:

   My brothers and myself *went* to school …
   Father *was making out* by killing pigs …
   We *had to get* them as white as a board …

   b What does the writer's choice of words tell you about him?

3 The writer uses a regional dialect term on line 13. Write it down and then explain in your own words what you think this means.

Advice   A regional dialect term is a word or phrase which might be used in one part of the country but which isn't part of standard English. It may be an expression which is still used today; or it may have died out. Just look at the context and try to work out from that what you think the writer means.

4 The writer describes some tasks which are unpleasant – for example, scraping pigs' insides and eating blackbird pie. He writes about these events in quite an impersonal way, without emotion. How does his use of language help to create an impersonal style? Think about:

   ● his use of vocabulary

   ● the style of his sentences

   ● his use of pronouns like *I*.

Advice Look at the way the writer uses factual words. There are no emotive adjectives like *unpleasant*, *horrible*, or *sickening*. Find some examples of more neutral words he uses.

Notice how he uses short sentences – such as at the end of the first paragraph. How do these create a factual tone?

Look at the writer's use of the pronoun *I*. How much does he use it? Is his style deeply personal, or does the passage seem more like a description in which he is not too involved?

5 The writer uses the more formal word *asset* to describe the Big House in the final paragraph. Explain what this word means. The sentences around it will help you.

6 The writer is looking back to memories of his childhood. Apart from the dates, what clues are there in the language that the passage is set in the past?

In particular, look for:

- any old or unfamiliar words

- verb forms which tell us that the events happened in the past.

Advice Don't just look at vocabulary. Remember that verbs and adverbs are used by writers to show the reader when events happened.

Verbs can be in the past, present, or future tense. Look for examples that this text is written in the past tense.

Writing

The text has many of the obvious features of autobiographical writing. How would it work differently if told in the third person ('Ronald … he … his family … they …'), as the opening of a novel? Try retelling the story of Ronald Blythe's early life using some of the style features of fiction.

- Use the past tense.

- Use dialogue to add variety to the text.

Then write a paragraph describing how you went about changing the extract, and what you think the effect of your changes was. How does your version feel different to Ronald Blythe's original?

Newspaper articles

Newspaper reporting aims to give us information and to help us understand a story in the news. Journalism has been described as 'writing in a hurry', but it is also intended to help us *read* in a hurry – giving us the main facts at the start of the article (and in the headline), before adding detail during the rest of the text.

Remember that there are many different styles of newspaper articles. Some are designed chiefly to inform (news articles), some to entertain (features articles). Those appearing in tabloid newspapers, such as *The Sun*, *The Mirror*, or *The Express* will probably have a less formal style than those in broadsheets like *The Independent*, *The Times*, or *The Guardian*.

Genre sample

To practise making more detailed comments about the language of texts, read the text below, and think what you would say about its layout, tone, vocabulary and sentence structure. Then look at the comments on the next page.

THURSDAY, MAY 28, 1998

THE DAILY TELEGRAPH

Teenager Owen scores a record

By Sebastien Berger

MICHAEL OWEN became the youngest player ever to score for England yesterday after recovering from being kicked in the head by the Moroccan goalkeeper in a 1-0 victory in Casablanca.

Owen, 18 years and 164 days, had been brought on in the first half as substitute for the injured Ian Wright and said later that his goal was all he could remember of the match.

Comments

What could you say about the layout?

The headline is designed to catch our attention and to tell us the bare facts of the story. The paragraphs are fairly short to keep our eyes moving quickly down the page.

What could you say about the tone?

The tone is informative and factual. The writer crams as much information as possible into each sentence – probably too much, in fact. The first sentence gives us the whole story: it is known as a topic sentence. A newspaper report usually begins with one of these. The writer seems pleased about the news: he makes Owen seem even more heroic by stressing the fact that he'd been 'kicked in the head'.

What could you say about the vocabulary?

The article uses the vocabulary of football – *player, kicked, goalkeeper, substitute,* and so on. The vocabulary is straightforward and easy to follow. The writing is not particularly descriptive: instead the writer just aims to give us the main facts of the story. (Background details, if they appeared at all, would come later in the story, not near the beginning.) As in most journalism, people are labelled: 'Owen, *18 and 164 days...*'; 'the *Moroccan* goalkeeper'; 'the *injured* Ian Wright'. This allows the writer to compress as much information into as small a space as possible.

What could you say about the sentence structure?

The sentences are complex, carrying lots of detail. The writer uses the past tense – *became, had been brought* – plus adverbs like *yesterday* to tell us when the news took place.

Review

The text actually feels overloaded with information, as if the writer expects each sentence to carry too many facts. The effect is an informative style which – even in two sentences – has told us the main details of the story.

Going further

Now look at another newspaper article, to see in more detail how news reporters use language to hold and keep the reader's attention.

Newspaper articles – the language of reporting

The newspaper report below tells the dramatic story of a runaway lorry.

MONDAY, MAY 11, 1998   THE DAILY TELEGRAPH

M1 police clear 20-mile path for runaway lorry

1 Lorry driver reports accelerator jammed on at 70mph heading south on M1 at junction 10

2 Five police cars escort lorry and clear road ahead

3 Driver crashes lorry into barrier after Scratchwood Services

By Barbie Dutter

A runaway lorry hurtled down the M1 with five police cars clearing its path after the accelerator pedal became stuck at 70mph yesterday.

Michael Rayner, the driver of the articulated tipper truck, dialled 999 from his mobile phone when he realized he was powerless to stop.

As the lorry sped towards London, five patrol cars formed an emergency escort with the Hertfordshire police helicopter flying overhead sending loud-hailer warnings to other drivers.

The drama continued for 20 miles – with two more police cars joining the escort along the way – with Mr Rayner snaking from lane to lane to avoid other vehicles. Finally he brought the truck to a halt by careering into a crash barrier.

Mr Rayner, 26, of Potters Bar, Herts, alerted police shortly before 11am at junction 10. For 20 minutes, officers debated how to deal with the problem and made suggestions to the driver.

The idea of simply turning off the engine was ruled out at first because it would affect the power-steering and make the driver lose control.

Mr Rayner said: 'It was a bit frightening to discover I was doing 80 miles per hour in a 38-ton lorry with no way of slowing down.

'The police just got everything off the road for me. I was in the fast lane, on the hard shoulder, anywhere I could get through and where I had a clear path. At the same time they were talking to me and advising me.'

He said the situation reached crisis point when officers told him there was only a short stretch of motorway remaining – with a roundabout at the end.

'It was decided I should get on to the hard shoulder and turn off the engine, which is what I did. The only trouble was a car had pulled over on to the hard shoulder.

'I could see the car in my path and I could see one or two children inside and that is why I had to steer into the crash barrier. When the driver saw me approaching, he was off like a shot.'

The lorry came to a halt near the Scratchwood services, tearing up a large section of the crash barrier. Mr Rayner was shaken but unhurt.

Acting duty inspector Jerry Bartlett, of Hertfordshire police said of the driver: 'It was basically down to his expertise and his bravery in actually forcing the truck to stop.'

---

1 As in most newspaper reports, this one begins with a topic sentence which tells us the main facts about the event. Which word in the first sentence gives the strongest sense of excitement to the story? Write it down, and then write a sentence explaining why.

Advice There are several possible choices: *runaway*, *hurtled*, *clearing*. You can pick any word you like, as long as you can explain your choice in a sentence. Try to show why the word creates a feeling of excitement.

2 The newspaper story is told in short paragraphs, most of them one sentence long. Why do you think this is?

3 Look at the way the writer has written paragraph 9 ('He said the situation...').

a What effect does the dash have before the last six words?

b The writer uses reported speech ('He said the situation was...') rather than direct speech ('He said, "The situation was..."'). Write down one reason why the writer might have decided to do this.

Advice Reported speech reports what a person says, rather than giving his exact words. If the paragraph used direct speech it would read like this: 'He said, "The situation reached crisis point when officers told me there was only a short stretch of motorway remaining – with a roundabout at the end."' Notice the change of the pronoun from *him* to *me.* Can you feel how the effect is different from the reported speech version?

Look at where this paragraph falls within the newspaper report – it may give you a clue to why the writer chose to use reported speech.

4 Look at the word *affect,* in paragraph 6. How is the meaning of this word different from *effect*? Try to write a short definition of each word, plus two sentences in which they appear.

5 Look at paragraph 7 ('Mr Rayner said …'). The writer uses inverted commas (speech marks) to show the driver's words, but she doesn't put inverted commas at the end of the paragraph. Why is this?

6 Because this is a piece of news reporting, the writer does not say directly what she thinks of the driver Michael Rayner. Can you find any clues from the passage which show the writer's opinion of Mr Rayner?

Advice

Look at the way the writer shows how serious the situation is, and how dangerous. What does this suggest about her attitude to the driver? Look also at the way the police describe the driver. The writer quotes their words. What does this also show about her opinion of him?

Writing

Like most newspaper articles, this one tells a story using the third person ('she/he …'), short paragraphs to keep our interest, and quotations from various people who were involved ('Mr Rayner said …'). What if it were written as a diary entry by Michael Rayner rather than a newspaper report? How would you expect the use of language to be different?

Retell the story of the runaway lorry by writing Michael Rayner's diary. You might use notes rather than full sentences; use the first person ('I…'); write about what you noticed, rather than the view of other drivers or the police.

(If you want to remind yourself of the style and language features of diary entries before you begin to write, turn to pages 68–69.)

Then write a paragraph describing the changes you have made to the original story in retelling it through a diary. Be as precise as you can about the language choices you have made.

Polemical writing

Polemical writing is writing which argues a case. It is designed to challenge your views and make you change your mind. You find it in leaflets, newspapers, magazines, and essays.

Genre sample

Keith Waterhouse has written columns in the *Daily Mail* newspaper since 1986, and he is well-known for his strong opinions. Here he attacks the way computers are used in libraries.

To practise making more detailed comments about the language of polemical texts, cover the comments section opposite, read the text, and think what you would say about the tone, vocabulary, and sentence structure which the writer uses.

Anyone who uses the public libraries knows that they are obsessed with computerization. Where once you had a neat card index in a polished mahogany nest of filing cabinets, you now have an electronic slum of sprawled printouts and scattered microfiches. Doubtless the computer is enormously useful to librarians wishing to check that the book they have not got is equally unavailable in other branches, but I don't see why it has to be inflicted on the customer. The fact is that most electronic gadgetry is the enemy of literature...

Keith Waterhouse,
Shelf-room for Reading

Comments

What could you say about the tone?

Keith Waterhouse's tone is confident, putting across controversial views without trying to defend them. He gives the impression that everyone would agree with him, when he states that 'Anyone who uses the public libraries knows…'. He uses sarcasm to add to his argument, with his joke about librarians checking that the book is 'equally unavailable in other branches'. He is very assertive: 'The fact is…' (even though it is actually an opinion). He makes the reader feel involved in the argument by use of the pronoun *you*.

What could you say about the vocabulary?

Waterhouse chooses words which will help him win his argument. He makes the days of card index systems sound attractive with vocabulary like *polished* (suggesting high standards) and *nest* (suggesting cosiness). He makes computers sound negative with words like *slum, sprawled* and *scattered*. The alliteration (repetition of first-sounds) emphasizes his harsh, dismissive attitude even more.

What could you say about the sentence structure?

Waterhouse's sentences are complex, but sound like someone speaking – for example: 'but I don't see why it has to be inflicted on the customer'. The use of the verb form *don't* makes the argument seem more personal than *do not* would have done. Writing in the present tense makes his argument all the more powerful and immediate.

Review

The text uses humour to make a serious point. It is happy to poke fun at librarians in order to show what libraries should really be like. The writer uses various techniques to involve the reader, aiming to carry us along with his argument so that we agree with his point of view.

Going further

Now look at another piece of polemical writing, and see how its author uses language to convince us of her message.

Susan Stranks, a former presenter on children's television, believes strongly that children should be given high quality radio programmes. Here she argues her case in *The Radio Magazine*. Read the passage and then answer the questions which follow.

The RADIO Magazine   The UK Radio Industry Newsweekly

The BBC is axing Children's Radio!

So it's finally happened! The BBC has killed off Children's Radio and will bury the shrivelled remains under extra episodes of The Archers – according to JAMES BOYLE's new RADIO 4 schedules, starting next April.

Let's examine the lame excuses for pushing children out of Radioland.

'Kids don't want radio… they only like TV and pop music!'

Kids both want and need radio and it should certainly be there to entertain, inform and educate them. They would flock to it, if it were appetizingly served, but the BBC has lost the will and the talent to reach children through this unique and most accessible medium and a single half hour hidden away on Sunday evening with no repeats and no promotion, however well produced, is not the way to do it.

'They can always buy tapes!'

Adults can buy tapes… they also like listening to radio.

'Youngsters use the adult sports and pop channels'

Youngsters are useful to top up adult ratings.

'We tried stories but they're not interested. You can't force kids to listen!'

No sirs you can't force them. Most kids prefer burgers and pop but to get them to eat fresh fruit and vegetables you dice them up into bite-sized chunks, you coat them with sugar and spice or you sandwich them between stuff they do enjoy. You add surprise, reward and street cred. And you sell 'em hard!

Millions are spent on selling radio to grown-ups. The BBC sold '5 Live' very hard to its target of young adult males, with £1.2m on advertising in the first year. Not much went on the kids' programmes which used to be on R5, yet they were listened to regularly by children and adults together – an achievement which the BBC apparently views as a failure.

The Corporation complains that the little drama spot on R4 only reaches 3,000 of its 'target' 7 – 10 year olds, but 200,000 adults also tune in. How dare grown-ups share our wonderful heritage of classic and popular children's literature! Make them listen to *The Archers* instead.

Dumb down adult listeners if you must but don't drag the children under with them.

Literacy is at an all time low, with thousands of 11 year olds in Summer crammers to improve their reading before they enter secondary school. One in five of Britain's pre-school children has speech delay, which can seriously inhibit schooling and social integration. Teachers and parents express grave concern that children don't listen, won't sit still and can't concentrate, while UK education standards fall increasingly short of other developed countries. For the world's leading public service broadcaster to axe children's radio when it is most needed is a national disgrace.

Humans need listening for the normal development of language, communication, imagination and motor skills, and radio can support and reinforce the difficult work of parents, carers and teachers in raising and educating the next generation. It can also give kids lots of fun.

In over 220 UK radio stations, not one is for children. Un-served as customers, Britain's young citizens are nonetheless paraded in tabloid style 'adult targeted' formats as sex objects, thugs, truants, drug and alcohol addicts, and educational failures, who are a trial to their parents, schools and society. The grim message is 'You have to be sad or bad to get noticed!'

What can be done? The spare 225 kHz Long Wave band should be developed into a brand new service for Children & Schools, using mid-week lottery funds earmarked for education. Such a network would play a key role in the learning support system the Government is nurturing in partnership with the private sector. This intelligent and timely use of public resources to serve national needs could well prove the most positive influence on education since the Open University.

Susan Stranks

Word bank   **James Boyle** – the controller of BBC Radio 4
5 Live – the BBC's news and sports channel

1 Look closely at Susan Stranks' first sentence. She uses three techniques to make the reader want to read on:

- starting with *So*

- using the pronoun *it*

- using an exclamation mark at the end of the sentence.

How do these three techniques get the reader involved?

Advice Remember that a pronoun usually refers back to a noun (e.g 'The cat saw the sausage and ate it' – *it* refers back to the noun *sausage*). Now look at the way the writer uses the word *it* in her first sentence.

2 Look at the opening to the second paragraph. The writer uses the word *Let's*, meaning *Let us*. Why do you think she uses the pronoun *us* rather than *me*?

3 The writer uses both formal and informal language in her text. The informal language makes it sound as if she is speaking to her audience, rather than writing. Write down an example of language from lines 32–39 which is closer to spoken than written language.

Advice Look for examples of informal language – expressions we might use in everyday conversation and words that have been shortened to sound more informal.

4 The writer uses the imperative verb form in a one-sentence paragraph, to tell the reader what should be done.

a Write down the sentence.

b Underline the words in the sentence which are alliterative (i.e. they all start with the same letter).

c Do you think this alliteration makes the sentence more effective? Say why.

5 Sometimes the writer uses the word *children*; sometimes she says *kids*. Why do you think she varies her usage in this way?

6 We get a very strong sense of what the writer thinks should be done, but she never uses the first person ('I think') in her writing. What effect does this have?

Advice   Writing *I think* would suggest that these are the writer's opinions. If you leave this phrase out, what impression does it give? What impression do you think the writer is aiming to create here?

7 Look at the early part of the article where the writer uses a certain structure to help argue her case. She uses quotations/comments, and then gives her own opinion. Does this approach work? Does it make her case more persuasive, or does it make the argument feel disjointed? Say what you thought of it, and why.

Writing

Susan Stranks uses a range of arguments in her article. Can you summarize what they are? Working on a sheet of A4, produce a summary of her key points, under these headings:

What is wrong with radio at the moment

Why children need radio

What should be done

Use bullet points, rather than paragraphs, to show that you can summarize the main points.

Diaries

Diaries are usually not written for publication. Diary-writers are often just recording their own thoughts and feelings for themselves. The style of writing in diaries is therefore very personal.

Genre sample

This extract from playwright Alan Bennett's diaries gives an account of an elderly woman who moves into a caravan at the bottom of his garden. He refers to her as Miss S.

To practise making more detailed comments about the language of diaries, cover the comments section opposite, read the text, and think what you would say about the tone, sentence structure and vocabulary which the author uses.

> **February 1981.** Miss S. has flu, so I am doing her shopping. I wait every morning by the side window of the van and, with the dark interior and her grimy hand holding back the purple curtain, it is as if I am at the confessional. The chief items this morning are ginger nuts ('very warming') and grape juice...
>
> **February 1983.** A. telephones me in Yorkshire to say that the basement is under three inches of water, the boiler having burst. When told that the basement has been flooded, Miss S's only comment is 'What a waste of water'.
>
> *Alan Bennett*

Comments

What could you say about the tone?

The tone is quite personal, using abbreviations like 'Miss S.' and 'A.'. This might be because the writer is recording details for himself and so does not need to write the names in full. Alternatively, it might be a way of protecting the identity of the people involved, after the diaries were published.

The tone is also quite affectionate – we can sense that the writer likes Miss S. He uses humour to suggest this – for example, comparing the process of getting her shopping list to attending confession in church. He pokes fun at her in a mild way.

What could you say about the sentence structure?

The sentences are written in a fairly informal style. The use of *so* in the very first sentence sounds like spoken rather than written English, though the phrase 'the boiler having burst' is more formal. One important feature of the grammar is the use of the present tense: 'I *am* doing her shopping ... A. *telephones* me from Yorkshire'. This creates a sense of immediacy – as if the events are happening now.

What could you say about the vocabulary?

The writer uses informal words, such as *flu, tattered*. He gives very specific details through his choice of words, such as *ginger nuts* and *grape juice*. (If he had used the words *biscuits* and *fruit juice* instead, what would have been the effect?) The writer also uses adjectives to help create a visual impression – for example, *grimy* and *dark*. These make the style more literary – as if the description belongs to a book rather than to everyday conversation.

Review

The text has many of the typical features of a diary, although some modern diaries are more informal than this. Like most diaries, it focuses on specific, individual people and events, often using abbreviations to save time. The use of the present tense makes the text seem very immediate.

Going further

Look at another diary, which uses a slightly different style to record far more dramatic and moving events.

Diaries – focus on personal writing

This diary was written by Sergeant Pexton,
a soldier in the Second World War.

War Diary, 1940

24 May. What a night. Rats running all over the place. Left Doullens for Albert. Sent off with one packet of English biscuits and half a tin of bully. Did 21 miles today, and very hot. They keep us away from all water and it is hell. Got to Albert at 8 p.m., just about all in, and went to aircraft works. Slept on the landing-ground. He'd made a mess of things here. Airplanes smashed up and the works badly smashed as well. I realize I'm a prisoner now all right. Just about fed up with everything. Wouldn't take much for me to make a break for it. It would be a quick way out anyway so long as he shot straight. Suppose I must not think that way and just carry on. It can't last for ever.

25 May. Had a very cold night at Albert and was glad to be on the road again. They gave us two packets of German biscuits and they taste awful. Black and bitter. Still they help to fill a terribly big hole. Lovely day but far too hot for marching, and in our condition too. Men are dropping out every mile now. Feet are in a terrible condition. I don't know how some of them march at all. Just the British spirit I expect. We're never beaten. Passed Delville Wood Cemetery today. Very big, and later passed Caterpillar Valley as well. Not as big but just as tidy. Cemeteries are all over this part of the country. Must have been some bother here in the last war all right. They look nice but I hope I don't end up in one. Arrived at the field and find this place is called Flers. Had a big thunderstorm just before arriving and got nice and wet. Everything wet to sleep on so I expect another lovely night.

26 May. The worst night yet. Left here for Cambrai and they gave us one biscuit on marching out. What a march. Will never understand how I did it, but here I am in the French barracks at last. There must be 30,000 of us on the road now. French mostly slept on the square although it was pouring with rain. We are that hungry we can't feel the wet. Germans say the war will be over in one month. I wonder.

Sergeant L D Pexton

Christina Dodwell　　　　　　　*The Long Bus Ride*

The next morning as I strolled out to find breakfast in the bazaar I saw two monkeys and a porcupine sitting beside a man who was doing a juggling act. But as soon as his concentration was established the monkeys began teasing the porcupine by grabbing his unprotected parts, and the juggler had to collapse his act to rescue the poor old porcupine.

Later I saw the same man talking to someone leading a large brown bear on a chain. They showed me their act, which was to persuade a small boy to put his neck in the bear's mouth. Actually I don't think the bear had enough teeth left to do any damage.

Word bank　　**ally** – friend
Baluchi – someone who comes from Baluchistan
corrugated – uneven
synchronized – moving in time with one another

1 Look again at the first sentence. The writer could have written a simple sentence: 'The bus waited a long time.' What effect does her opening sentence achieve?

Advice

Think about the use of repetition – of *didn't*, *leave*, and *hours*.
Think of what the writer is saying and how this repetition adds to the effect.
Think also about the length and the structure of her sentence.

2 In the third sentence the writer says, 'That blew my chances of getting across the longer half of the desert by night.'

The verb *blew* is quite an informal word.

a Think of a more formal verb that the writer might have used.

b Write down why the writer might have chosen to use the more informal word.

3 The passage takes place over two days. How does the writer use discourse markers to create an impression of time passing?

Advice

Discourse markers help a reader to find her way about a text – to know where she is. Discourse markers in this passage include *after*, *finally*, *there*, *the next*, *later*. Don't just list them – say what effect they have, for example, 'Use of "finally" at the start of a paragraph shows that a long time has passed. It tells the reader that we have moved forward in time.'

4 List some of the adjectives the writer uses when describing the bus, then explain how they make the description of the bus particularly vivid.

5 Look at the last sentence. It begins with the word *actually*. Try to explain what the effect of this word is.

Advice If you find this difficult, try to imagine the same sentence without the word *Actually*. How would it have felt different?

6 Would you describe Christina Dodwell's style as formal or informal, or a mixture of both? Write down your opinion, and use examples from the text to support it.

Writing

Christina Dodwell's account tells us:

- about the places she visits
- about the people she sees
- about her own feelings.

To do this, she uses both descriptive and narrative styles of writing. But what if her adventures in Baluchistan were going to feature in a short newspaper report in a local newspaper? How would the style and the content change?

Write a 200-word interview with Christina Dodwell as if you were a journalist on a local newspaper in the area of Britain where she lives.

Remember to:

- change from the first person ('I') to the third person ('she')
- cut down the amount of descriptive detail
- quote her own words to make it sound like an interview: for example, Christina Dodwell says, 'I was impressed by the way men automatically helped each other and women gave their water to those who needed it more.'
- make your style as entertaining and dramatic as possible, so that readers want to read on.

If you want to remind youself of the style and language features of newspaper reports before you begin to write, turn to pages 57–58.

Travel writing – writing about action

Travel writer Redmond O'Hanlon describes a dangerous journey by canoe through rapids in Borneo, South America.

Redmond O'Hanlon

Into the Heart of Borneo

We entered a wide reach of foaming water. The choppy river-waves, snatching this way and that, had ripped caves of soil out of the banks, leaving hundreds of yards of overhang on either side. There was an ominous noise of arguing currents ahead. The rapids-preamble – the white water, the moving whirlpools, the noise ahead – was longer and louder than it ought to have been.

With the canoe pitching feverishly, we rounded a sweeping bend; and the reason for the agitated river became obvious. The Green Heave ahead was much higher than any we had met. There was a waterfall to the left of the river-course, a huge surging over a ledge. The way to the right was blocked by thrown-up trees and piles of roots that had been dislodged upstream, torn out in floods, and tossed aside here against a line of rocks. There was, however, one small channel through; a shallow rapid, dangerously close to the main rush of water, but negotiable. It was separated from the torrent by three huge boulders.

Keeping well clear of the great whirlpool beneath the waterfall, Leon brought the boat to the base of this normal-size rapid. Dana, James and I made our way carefully up with the bow-rope.

Redmond O'Hanlon

Dana held the lead position on the rope; I stood behind him and James behind me. We pulled, Leon and Inghai pushed. The boat moved up and forward some fifteen feet and then stuck. Leon and Inghai walked up the rapid, and, hunching and shoving, rolled small rocks aside to clear a channel. We waited on the lip of the rock above, pulling on the rope to keep the long boat straight. At last Leon and Inghai were ready. But the channel they had had to make was a little closer to the waterfall. To pull straight we must move to our right. Dana pointed to our new positions.

It was only a stride or two. But the level of the river-bed suddenly dipped, long since scooped away by the pull of the main current. James lost his footing, and, trying to save himself, let go of the rope. I stepped across to catch him, the rope bound round my left wrist, snatching his left hand in my right. His legs thudded into mine, tangled, and then swung free, into the current, weightless, as if a part of him had been knocked into outer space. His hat came off, hurtled past his shoes, spun in an eddy, and disappeared over the lip of the fall.

His fingers were very white; and slippery. He bites his fingernails; and they could not dig into my palm. He simply looked surprised; his head seemed a long way from me. He was feeling underwater with his free arm, impossibly trying to grip a boulder with his other hand, to get a purchase on a smooth and slimy rock, a rock polished smooth, for centuries, by perpetual tons of rolling water.

His fingers bent straighter, slowly, edging out of mine, for hour upon hour — or so it felt, but it must have been seconds. His arm rigid, his fingertips squeezed out of my fist. He turned in the current, spread-eagled. Still turning, but much faster, he was sucked under; his right ankle and shoe were bizarrely visible above the surface; he was lifted slightly, a bundle of clothes, of no discernible shape, and then he was gone.

'Boat! Boat!' shouted Dana, dropping the rope, bounding down the rocks of the rapid at the side, crouched, using his arms like a baboon.

'Hold the boat! Hold the boat!' yelled Leon.

James's bald head, white and fragile as an owl's egg, was sweeping round in the whirlpool below, spinning, bobbing up and down in the foaming water, each orbit of the current carrying him within inches of the black rocks at its edge.

Word bank

maelstrom – whirlpool
perpetual – constant
preamble – early part

1 The opening paragraphs use active verbs and participles to describe the drama of the scene.

  a For each of the words below, say what picture they create in your mind:

    snatching (participle)
    ripped (verb)
    pitching (participle)
    torn out (verb)

  b For each example, see if you can think of another word the writer might have used.

2 The writer frequently uses adjectives to add detail to his nouns – for example:

wide reach
foaming water
ominous noise
huge surging

  a Find three nouns the writer uses without adjectives.

  b Say whether you think he over-uses adjectives in the text.

3 The opening paragraphs use many adjectives. Then, from paragraph 3 onwards, the writer uses fewer adjectives and more verbs. What effect does this have?

4 One of the explorers, James, is swept off his feet by the force of the water; the writer describes how he tries to hold on to the other man. Everything happens fast – but to the writer the events seem to take hours. How does the style of the writing in paragraphs 6 and 7 (from 'His fingers were...' to '...he was gone') reflect this?

In your answer, try to comment on:

- the length of the sentences

- the amount of description.

5 Look again at the last paragraph. How does the writer use language to show how much danger James is in?

Advice

Look at the choice of verbs and the way the writer lists them.
Look at the simile used to describe James's head.

Look at the adjective used to describe the rocks – how does this suggest trouble?

Writing

Does the power of this text come from the description?
Take the first sentence:

> We entered a wide reach of open water.

Take out the adjectives and it reads like this:

> We entered a reach of water.

Does the text already feel less powerful? Do we feel that we visualize it less well? Do we feel less involved?

Choose two paragraphs and rewrite them by removing the descriptive details – in particular, the adjectives and adverbs. Reduce the text to its bare elements. Then read your version back. How does it feel different? Write a paragraph describing the differences you notice.

Information texts

There are all kinds of information texts – from reference books like encyclopedias to leaflets, guide books, instruction sheets and recipes.

Genre sample

This is an entry from an encyclopedia. To practise making more detailed comments about the language of information texts, read the extract and think what you would say about its structure, its tone and the vocabulary the writer has used. Then turn over and read the comments on the next page.

Maldives, Republic of A small country in the Indian Ocean, to the SW of Sri Lanka. It consists of a large number of small coral islands, grouped in atolls, of which just over 200 are inhabited ...
Official language: Divehi. Official religion: Islam. Official currency: Maldivian rupee of 100 larees. Area: 298 sq km (115 sq mi). Population (1983): 168,000. Capital and main port: Malé.

Macmillan Encyclopedia

Comments

What could you say about the tone?

The tone is highly impersonal – we get no sense of who the writer is. The idea is to make the reader focus on the factual information.

What could you say about the vocabulary?

This is quite technical, with abbreviations like *SW* to make the reading process quicker and more efficient. The aim is to inform rather than to entertain.

What could you say about the sentence structure?

Much of the text is not written in sentences. The first sentence, for example, contains no verb. Later sentences are actually phrases. This allows the writer to give as much essential information in as few words as possible.

What could you say about the discourse structure?

The text starts with the more global information – main overall details. Then it gets into the specific details.

Review

All information texts vary, but this is typical of an encyclopedia entry – with its heavy emphasis on factual details and statistics, and its impersonal, neutral tone.

Going further

Now look at a more complex information text, which aims not only to inform, but also to persuade.

Information texts – focus on instruction

Read the passage about fire safety. It is taken from a booklet produced for children by Norfolk and Norwich Hospital. Then answer the questions.

RED ALERT – FIRE AND ITS CONSEQUENCES

"Sometimes fires will start accidentally so you need to know how to react to them."

Smoke Alarms

One of the most frightening things about fire is that we often don't know that it is happening. By making sure that our families fit smoke alarms we can ensure an early warning system which will give us extra minutes to escape from the house.

Smoke alarms are gadgets about the size of an adult's hand. They are fitted to ceilings and make a loud alarm noise to warn us if they detect any smoke. Alarms can be bought from DIY shops, hardware stores and some supermarkets. They cost between £3 and £10. It is important that your smoke alarms have the British Standard Kite Mark on them. This shows that they are good quality alarms.

It is important that we have at least one smoke alarm on each storey. Don't put alarms in or near the bathroom or kitchen as the steam or burnt toast etc will set them off continually.

When your parents fit a smoke alarm remind them:

1 Fit it as close as possible to the centre of the room.

2 Fit it where it can be heard upstairs and downstairs – better still fit two!

3 Check the alarm battery once a week by pressing the test button.

4 Change the alarm battery once a year and vacuum the dust from the inside of the alarm.

RED ALERT – FIRE AND ITS CONSEQUENCES

"Have you ever burnt your hand on the steam from a kettle or on a heater?
If so you will know how much burns hurt"

Doctors and nurses describe burns in different ways depending how bad they are:

First Degree Burns are the kind of burns that you will probably have come across. The burnt skin goes red and needs to be cooled with water.

Second Degree Burns are when the skin becomes red and blistered. These are more serious than first degree burns and, as soon as they have been cooled with water, they should be seen by a doctor or nurse.

Third Degree Burns are the most serious ones. Again these should be cooled with water and seen by a doctor. Do not remove any clothing from the burnt area of the body.

If you or a member of your family gets burnt:

1 Place the burn under cold, slow-running water for at least 15 minutes.

2 So long as clothing etc is not stuck to the skin, remove any jewellery or tight clothing.

3 Cover the burn with cling film.

4 See a doctor about the burn.

REMEMBER
1. **Do not touch blistered skin.**
2. **Never treat burns with ointments or sticking plasters.**

1 Look closely at the first sentence of the text, under the heading 'Smoke Alarms'.

   a How can you tell that it is aimed at children?

   b Why do you think the writer uses the pronoun *we* rather than *you*?

2 Some of the sentences in the text are designed to give information ('Smoke alarms are gadgets about the size of an adult's hand'). Some are designed to give instructions ('Fit it as close as possible to the centre of the room').

What differences in structure do you notice between the sentences which give information and the sentences which give instruction?

In particular, look at:

- the length of the different types of sentences

- the subject of the sentence

- where the verb appears.

Advice Sentences which give instructions are sometimes called imperative sentences. One of the main grammatical points about these sentences is that they usually don't have an obvious subject. Instead of saying, 'You should fit it as close as possible', they say, 'Fit it as close...'. This makes the sentence sound much more direct, like an order. Notice also that the verb is usually placed at the beginning of an imperative sentence: 'Fit it...'

3 The writer uses some words which will be easily understood by children, such as *frightening*. Write down any words which you are surprised to see in a text aimed at children – words which seem too complex. Try to find three examples.

4 Look at the way the writer uses comparative and superlative adjectives:

adjective	**comparative**	**superlative**
serious	more serious	most serious

For each of the adjectives below, write down a comparative and superlative form:

a bad
b cold
c tight
d blistered
e frightening

5 Look more closely at the way the writer uses elisions, such as *don't*. At other times he uses the more formal version, *do not*. Look for some examples in the text. Then write a sentence saying why you think the writer sometimes uses elided forms and, at other times, separate words.

Writing

Some readers think the text is probably too difficult for very young children: they would have problems understanding all parts of it. How would you communicate the message of the text to children aged 5-6 as a poster? Remember that they will only just have started to read, so the vocabulary needs to be very simple. Remember not to use too many words in each sentence. Have a go, on one side of A4 paper, at producing a poster which will show these young children the dangers of fire and how to cope with burns. Don't spend too long on the design of the poster – it's the language level which is the real key to being successful with this task.

Then write a paragraph explaining how you changed the text to suit a younger audience, and reflecting on how well your finished poster works.

Speeches

Speeches remain a powerful way of informing and persuading people – in school, in battle, and in parliament. A well-crafted speech can stir our emotions and make us support the speaker's point of view.

Genre sample

In 1986, the Space Shuttle *Challenger* exploded shortly after take-off, killing its crew. The explosion was watched by millions of TV viewers who had switched on to see the launch. It was the worst accident in the history of space exploration. Shortly afterwards, US President Ronald Reagan delivered the following speech.

To practise making more detailed comments about the language of speeches, read the text and think what you would say about its tone and vocabulary, and the sentence structures it uses.

We mourn seven heroes – Michael Smith, Dick Scobee, Judith Resnik, Ronald McNair, Ellison Onizuka, Gregory Jarvis and Christa McAuliffe. We mourn their loss as a nation, together.

To the families of the Seven: we cannot bear, as you do, the full impact of this tragedy – but we feel the loss, and we are thinking about you so very much. Your loved ones were daring and brave and they had that special grace, that special spirit that says, 'Give me a challenge and I'll meet it with joy'. They had a hunger to explore the universe and discover its truths. They wished to serve and they did – they served us all.

Speech by Ronald Reagan, written by Peggy Noonan

Introduction

What could you say about the tone?

The tone is formal and sombre, with words suggesting respect and honour. The writer speaks on behalf of America – 'We mourn their loss as a nation, together' – making the reader (or listener) feel involved. The writer also addresses the families of the heroes directly – 'To the families of the Seven', with a capital 's' on Seven to show their special status.

What could you say about the vocabulary?

The words are full of emotional power and feelings of pride and honour: *heroes, tragedy, daring, brave, grace*. The words are abstract, referring to concepts like *challenge* and *truths*. The people who died are described as *heroes, loved ones* and *the Seven*. The writer avoids using the words *death* or *crash*, and instead writes at a more emotional level.

What could you say about the sentence structure?

The writer uses long sentences to build up rhythms in the speech – the list of the heroes' names, and the coordination of phrases with *and*: 'Your loved ones were daring and brave and they had...'. The flowing rhythm adds to the emotional effect of the speech, carrying us along, where a more disjoined style might not have the same effect. The repetition of elements – 'they wished to serve and they did – they served us all' – also adds to the emotional power, emphasizing the service of the heroes on behalf of the nation.

Review

The speech is a powerful piece of persuasive writing, using vocabulary and grammar to provoke an emotional response from the audience.

Going further

Now look at another very famous speech, made following a tragic death. It is unusual because it is addressed both to the people listening, and to the subject of the speech.

Speeches – focus on emotive language

Following the death of Princess Diana in August 1997, her brother, Earl Spencer, delivered a powerful speech at her funeral. This is the opening part…

Funeral Speech for Diana Princess of Wales

I stand before you today the representative of a family in grief, in a country in mourning before a world in shock.

We are all united not only in our desire to pay our respects to Diana but rather in our need to do so.

For such was her extraordinary appeal that the tens of millions of people taking part in this service all over the world via television and radio who never actually met her, feel that they, too, lost someone close to them in the early hours of Sunday morning. It is a more remarkable tribute to Diana than I can ever hope to offer her today.

Diana was the very essence of compassion, of duty, of style, of beauty. All over the world she was a symbol of selfless humanity, a standard-bearer for the rights of the truly downtrodden, a truly British girl who transcended nationality, someone with a natural nobility who was classless, who proved in the last year that she needed no royal title to continue to generate her particular brand of magic.

Today is our chance to say 'thank you' for the way you brightened our lives, even though God granted you but half a life. We will all feel cheated that you were taken from us so young and yet we must learn to be grateful that you came along at all.

Only now you are gone do we truly appreciate what we are now without and we want you to know that life without you is very, very difficult.

We have all despaired at our loss over the past week and only the strength of the message you gave us through your years of giving has afforded us the strength to move forward.

There is a temptation to rush to canonize your memory. There is no need to do so. You stand tall enough as a human being of unique qualities not to need to be seen as a saint. Indeed to sanctify your memory would be to miss out on the very core of your being, your wonderfully mischievous sense of humour with the laugh that bent you double, your joy for life transmitted wherever you took your smile, and the sparkle in those unforgettable eyes, your boundless energy which you could barely contain.

But your greatest gift was your intuition, and it was a gift you used wisely. This is what underpinned all your wonderful attributes. And if we look to analyse what it was about you that had such a wide appeal, we find it in your instinctive feel for what was really important in all our lives.

Without your God-given sensitivity, we would be immersed in greater ignorance at the anguish of AIDS and HIV sufferers, the plight of the homeless, the isolation of lepers, the random destruction of land mines.

Diana explained to me once that it was her innermost feelings of suffering that made it possible for her to connect with her constituency of the rejected.

And here we come to another truth about her. For all the status, the glamour, the applause, Diana remained throughout a very insecure person at heart, almost childlike in her desire to do good for others so she could release herself from deep feelings of unworthiness of which her eating disorders were merely a symptom.

The world sensed this part of her character and cherished her for her vulnerability, whilst admiring her for her honesty. The last time I saw Diana was on July the first, her birthday, in London, when typically she was not taking time to celebrate her special day with friends but was guest of honour at a charity fund-raising evening.

She sparkled of course, but I would rather cherish the days I spent with her in March when she came to visit me and my children in our home in South Africa. I am proud of the fact that apart from when she was on public display meeting President Mandela, we managed to contrive to stop the ever-present paparazzi from getting a single picture of her.

That meant a lot to her.

Earl Spencer

Word bank

canonize – make someone into a saint
constituency – area of special responsibility
paparazzi – Italian word meaning newspaper photographers
sanctify – make sacred

1 In the early parts of the speech, Earl Spencer refers to Diana as *she*. Later he calls her *you*. What effect does this change of pronouns have?

Advice Think about how your impression of Diana changes. When she is referred to as *you*, does the speech seem more personal? Does the use of the pronoun change the tone – does the speech become more or less private? Do you feel that you know Diana more at certain points in the speech because of this use of pronouns?

2 Look again at the first paragraph and notice the way the speech uses repetition of structures: 'a family *in* grief… a country *in* mourning… a world *in* shock.'

a Look at the first noun in each phrase ('family … country … world'). Do you notice a pattern developing in this choice of nouns? What is it?

b Look at the abstract noun at the end of each phrase. What do they all have in common?

3 Part of the power of the speech comes from its use of repetition. Find two examples of the writer repeating words or phrases. Then, beneath each example, describe as precisely as you can what the writer is doing and what the effect is (for example: 'the writer repeats three abstract nouns; the effect is to emphasize the range of talents of the princess').

4 The speech is successful partly because it uses emotive vocabulary – words which carry emotional power, like *shock, strength, honesty*. Write down three other emotive words the writer uses.

5 Look at *paparazzi* in the penultimate sentence. What is the effect of using this word rather than *photographers*?

Tesco has been promoting a healthy balanced diet for 10 years, since Government reports recommended we cut down on fat (particularly saturated fat), sugar and salt, and increase the amount of fibre we eat. These changes are still needed to make our diets more healthy. The Chief Medical Officer, Dr Kenneth Calman has recently said:

'I am issuing a challenge to every person in the country to take a small step to improve their own health.'

Tesco has taken up the challenge and this leaflet helps you understand the issues with regard to fibre in the diet.

WHAT IS FIBRE?

INSOLUBLE

Fibre is made up of a number of complex substances which are all types of carbohydrate. They are only found in plants and come mainly from the plant cell walls. However, foods which are rich in fibre such as wholemeal bread, pasta, pulses and potatoes, provide more than just fibre in our diet. They also contain vitamins and minerals, are low in fat, and are good sources of starchy carbohydrate. Together with fruit and vegetables, we should be aiming to eat more of these foods.

WHY DO WE NEED FIBRE?

Fibre is an important part of our daily diet because it:
• stimulates the digestive system • helps prevent constipation • makes us feel full
• helps reduce the risk of digestive disorders • contributes few calories.

THERE ARE TWO TYPES OF FIBRE - INSOLUBLE AND SOLUBLE

INSOLUBLE FIBRE is found mainly in wheat products like wholemeal flour, bread and pasta, some breakfast cereals, bran and fibrous vegetables like carrots. It is important because it acts rather like a sponge when we eat it, soaking up moisture in the stomach and swelling up. This makes us feel full, leaving less room for the fatty sugary products, and stimulates the digestive system.

SOLUBLE FIBRE is found in significant amounts in virtually all fruits and vegetables. However, the richest sources of soluble fibre are pulses (e.g. red kidney beans, baked beans and lentils) and also products containing oats, barley or rye. There is some evidence to suggest that soluble fibre, particularly that found in oats, peas, beans and lentils, may help to reduce the level of cholesterol in the blood. This is most effective in combination with a diet which is low in fat, particularly saturated fat.

Genre sample

This leaflet from the supermarket Tesco aims to encourage its customers to add more fibre to their diet.

To practise making more detailed comments about the language of texts, cover the comments section below, read the text, and think what you would say about its layout, tone, vocabulary and sentence structure.

Comments

What could you say about the layout?
Look at the use of logos and colours, including the image of a human made up from food. These make the page eye-catching, encouraging us to read it.

What could you say about the tone?
The leaflet is factual and quite impersonal – for example, the writer uses the passive: 'Soluble fibre is found in …'; rather than 'You find soluble fibre in …' As a result the text feels more scientific and we feel less involved in it.

What could you say about the sentence structure?
The sentences are mostly quite long. The leaflet seems to be aimed at an audience whose reading skills are good. The text sometimes uses questions to involve the reader more – for example, 'How can we increase fibre in the diet?'
Notice the different types of text – the questions, the bullet points, the quotations, plus headings and subheadings. Again, this adds variety to the page.

What could you say about the vocabulary?
The leaflet uses some technical terms – carbohydrate, starch, saturated fat. Again, it is not talking down to the audience: it assumes that the reader understands these terms.

Review
The leaflet is not easy to read – partly because the text size is small and partly because it uses some technical vocabulary and complex sentences. But it is very informative.

Going further

Now look at another leaflet, with a strong persuasive message.

This leaflet is designed to encourage people to give up smoking.

Why does smoking affect the heart?

Tobacco smoke is packed with poisons that can damage the heart and blood vessels:

- Nicotine – an addictive poison, makes the heart beat faster, and makes blood pressure soar temporarily. It also increases the risk of blood clots.

- Carbon monoxide – a poisonous gas released when tobacco burns. Inhaled by the smoker, it dramatically cuts the amount of oxygen the blood can carry around the body and to the heart.

So when you smoke, your heart is having to work harder and is getting less oxygen.

How much at risk is the smoker?

Smoking dramatically increases the risk of developing heart disease, lung cancer and many other diseases. These diseases are not always fatal but can seriously affect your quality of life. Smoke and you're more likely to die before you retire. 40% of heavy smokers (those smoking over 20 cigarettes a day) die before retirement age, compared to only 15% of non-smokers.

Women are as much at risk as men of developing diseases from smoking – smoking-related diseases in women are still on the increase.

The risk of heart disease is dramatically increased for women who are over 35, smoke and who take the contraceptive pill. But now, thankfully, people are more aware of the health hazards and women, like men, are choosing to quit smoking. Why not join them?

What about the risk for the passive smoker?

Cigarettes give off two types of smoke – 'mainstream smoke' is filtered by the cigarette and inhaled by the smoker. The other type is sidestream smoke which goes directly from the end of the cigarette into the air. As it is not filtered it contains higher concentrations of harmful substances than the mainstream smoke. It is therefore potentially dangerous to non-smokers, especially when they are exposed to it for long periods of time.

Children who are exposed to their parents' sidestream smoke are more prone than other children to serious chest illnesses such as pneumonia, lung cancer and bronchitis. They are also more likely to smoke if their parents do.

The benefits of giving up

Give up and the risks decrease dramatically. Because nicotine is addictive this will be difficult and withdrawal symptoms such as irritability and restlessness can be experienced. These should only last a few weeks, however, and will be well worth the discomfort – 11 million people in Britain have given up, in most cases by will-power alone. If you do give up you should not only feel much fitter but your risk of developing heart disease will rapidly decrease during the first year. If you continue to be a non-smoker the risks will decrease so that, in time, the risks will be almost the same as they are for someone who has never smoked.

But there's more to quitting smoking than a healthy heart and healthy lungs. We can all spot smokers who quit – they're just so full of themselves! But with good reason. Until you kick the weed it's hard to appreciate, but it's a fantastic feeling. With food it's like having a veil lifted – you can really taste again, really enjoy it. As general fitness returns your body feels renewed, recharged, and as you continue to say NO to tobacco, it's a fantastic boost to your self esteem.

Help yourself to quit

1 Stop day – choose a day to stop and stop completely on that day.

2 Tell everyone you're stopping – this will give you support and encouragement to stick with it when you feel tempted to light up.

3 Take it a day at a time and each day try for just one more day.

4 Identify times when you particularly crave a cigarette and make sure you have something to occupy your hands (worry beads, a pencil to doodle with, sewing).

5 Ash cash – work out how much you're saving and plan how to spend it.

6 Think positively – you're a non-smoker, not a smoker who's given up. When you're offered a cigarette say 'No thanks, I don't smoke' – every time!

7 When you feel the urge to smoke, remember how well you've done so far and how hard it was to give up in the first place.

8 Not everyone succeeds the first time. It's a strong addiction, but don't give up trying.

9 Find out what's available locally. Ask your family doctor about the availability of techniques like nicotine chewing gum, stop-smoking groups, hypnosis, acupuncture, aversion therapy and relaxation classes or contact QUIT or ASH for a 'give-up' pack (see reverse for addresses).

1 Three of the four headings in the leaflet use questions rather than statements (for example, 'Why does smoking affect the heart?'). Why do you think the writer uses these?

2 Look at the fourth paragraph of the leaflet: 'So when you smoke, your heart is having to work harder and is getting less oxygen.'

   a Why do you think the writer uses the second person form here (*you* and *your*) rather than say, 'When people smoke, they …'?

   b What effect does the conjunction *So* have at the beginning of the sentence? How would the effect be different without it?

3 The writer uses a lot of adjective-noun structures (also called 'noun phrases') to give a feeling of detail – for example, *mainstream smoke, higher concentrations, harmful substances.* Find an example of a similar structure in the last paragraph.

4 Sometimes the writer's style is formal ('It is therefore potentially dangerous …'); sometimes it is more informal ('Until you kick the weed it's hard to appreciate').

   Look at the last two paragraphs on page 101. Write down one sentence which has a formal tone and one which has an informal tone.

   Describe what makes the tone in each one formal or informal.

Advice Remember that the tone is set partly by the vocabulary we use – *cigarette* is more formal than *fag*. Remember that elisions also create informality – *isn't* is more informal than *is not*.

Sentence structures can also create a different tone: complex sentences are often more formal, whereas compound sentences ('and … but … and') feel more like everyday speech and are therefore more informal.

Writing narratives

Introduction

A narrative is a story. In your class work you may find yourself writing a complete story; in a test, you're more likely to be asked to write just the opening. Whichever you do, always remember that the kind of writing you're doing will affect the grammar and language structures you use. If you're writing an action-packed story opening, you're more likely to choose simple sentences rather than complex ones, and you may not use many adjectives. On the other hand, a descriptive story opening which builds up atmosphere through lots of detail will usually include more adjectives and adverbs, plus similes and metaphors.

A good story opening will have:

- an intriguing situation which makes the reader want to read on
- a strong sense of setting – the reader will be able to visualize where the events take place
- a central character whom the reader finds interesting
- enough description to help the reader imagine the scene, but not so much that the story gets 'bogged down' in it
- interesting, precise vocabulary
- a variety of sentences to hold the reader's attention.

The next two activities (Tasks 1 and 2) will help you to practise writing narratives. Task 1 includes an 'Advice' panel to help you. Task 2 has no 'Advice' panel, so you can do this under test conditions.

Task 1

Look at this picture.

Who is this person?
What is she feeling?
Where is she?
What has just happened?
What will happen next?

Write the opening of a story which uses the photograph as a starting-point.

You should aim to:

● use an opening sentence which will capture the reader's attention and hint at what is going to happen

● describe the place where the story is set

● describe the thoughts and feelings of the main character

● introduce the main storyline – what happens next...?

Remember that you are only writing the opening.
You do not need to think of an ending to the story.

Advice

Spend some time planning your story. Brainstorm ideas about the character; where she is; what has just happened; what will happen next.

Think of a really dramatic opening sentence – such as: 'Susan Kramer knew that life would never be the same again'.

Use a variety of different sentence types: simple sentences for impact and clarity; complex and compound sentences to add detail.

Choose your vocabulary so that it helps the reader to see what is going on: for example, instead of writing 'Susan Kramer walked slowly', you could write 'Susan Kramer shuffled' – the choice of verb can add to the reader's impression of how she moves.

Use different narrative styles: some sentences which move the story on; some which are dialogue (the words people say); some which are description.

Remember that you can use flashbacks or breaks in the narrative to add to the effect.

Task 2
Read the opening of this mystery story.

There was something behind him. Alex knew it. As he shut the door, he felt his heart pumping fast. He reached in his pocket for the key...

Write the next part of the story. Try to write in a way that keeps the story moving and creates a strong sense of atmosphere.

In your opening you should:

- start with an opening sentence which captures the reader's attention and suggests what is going to happen next

- describe the scene where the story is set

- give a strong sense of the main character.

Writing letters

Introduction

Letters can serve a variety of purposes – for example, to communicate news, to complain, or to inform someone about something.

In tests you might be asked to write any kind of letter, so it is important to be clear about the purpose of your letter and the audience it is aimed at. Keep this in mind and you will get the style right. A letter to a friend will have a more informal feel than a letter to someone you don't know.

A good letter will:

- use the appropriate layout
- have a strong sense of audience – i.e. who it is being written to
- be clearly structured
- be accurate.

The next two activities (Tasks 3 and 4) will help you to practise writing letters. Task 3 includes an 'Advice' panel to help you. Task 4 has no 'Advice' panel, so you can do this under test conditions.

Task 3

Think about your school's uniform, if there is one. Imagine that you and many other students are unhappy with the current dress code at your school and you think it needs updating. If you do not currently have a uniform, imagine that you think there *should* be one.

Write a letter to your Headteacher saying why you think the uniform should be changed and how. Explain what the effect would be in school – and on the way the school is regarded by people in the community.

Aim to put your points across clearly and politely.

Advice Get the layout right – this is a formal letter. Write your address and the date in full; then the name of the Headteacher and school address. Use the correct sign-off – *Yours sincerely* (because you know the name of the Headteacher). Get the tone right – it is supposed to be quite formal. Choose your vocabulary carefully and avoid elisions (e.g. write *do not* rather than *don't*). Structure your ideas carefully, and remember to give reasons for your suggestions.

Task 4

Your local newspaper is looking for 'local heroes' – people who have achieved something, or made life better for other people.

You want to nominate a student from your own school. You have made the following notes about him:

Ben Last – 15
County-level swimmer
Up at 5 each day to train
Also helps with local disabled swimming group
Last Saturday in High Street – tackled mugger who had assaulted old man
Ben stopped mugger getting away until security officer from local shop, then police, arrived.

Write a letter to the newspaper nominating Ben Last.

In your letter, include the following details:

- who he is, plus some other factual information about him
- what he has achieved
- how you know him
- why you are nominating him.

Address your letter to:

J Ratcliff
Editor, The Mercury
16 The Street
Grantham
L32 2BS

Task 6

Read the following text in which a girl (Caroline Hardy) describes a car accident she witnessed. It has been written down as the girl said it.

Well it's always right busy at that time of the morning anyway, it must have been around 8.30 the rush-hour and the first thing I noticed was someone pressing horn really loud and a loud noise of brakes going on, the white car had er just just pulled out into the outside lane I think the driver can't have seen the Volvo because it just pulled out and then with the horn it suddenly pulled back in right over there and probably too much 'cos the driver came right across the lane and onto the verge the car hit the crash barrier and there was a huge shower of sparks but it stopped and the driver jumped out, he seemed fine actually really pale but okay and I said there's a Little Chef down there you could call the police from there and that's what he did

Imagine you are a police officer who has been called to the scene and you have to write a report on what happened.

In your report you should:

- arrange the facts into a sensible order and summarize them

- write in an appropriate way for a formal report, including using the third person, the past tense and reported speech.

Read the passage again before you start to write. The opening of the report has been done for you:

> The witness Caroline Hardy said that the accident occurred during the rush-hour...

Advice

Reported speech is a writing technique which allows us to state what someone said without actually quoting their words directly. Compare the effect:

Direct speech
The boy said, 'The house is on fire.'

Reported speech
The boy said that the house was on fire.

Reported speech drops the speech marks.
It usually adds the coordinating conjunction *that*.
It shifts the action to the past tense ('...the house *was* on fire.').

Task 7

Imagine you are a teacher who has organized a school exchange visit to Germany. Below are some of the notes which you made on the trip.

Write the notes up into a formal report for the headteacher of the school.

In your report you should:

- write in complete sentences
- link the points
- use an appropriate style and tone.

Notes – School exchange visit to Kiel

Generally very successful –
good weather – hot sunshine –
excellent behaviour of all students

Day trips to Hamburg and Berlin went very well

Samantha Taylor had bad asthma attack on second day –
left Ventolin behind so had to be taken to local hospital –
given oxygen (on ventilator) – then fine

Coach journey fine except for 2-hour delay at the ferry terminal
– cause not made clear

Driver helpful – good relationship with staff and students

Exchange placements went well – all students happy – Jon
Bromley very homesick for the first couple of days – you spoke
to his mother about this

Last-night party successful – students enjoyed it and many felt
upset to be coming back home

Writing leaflets

Introduction

Leaflets can be used to inform, entertain, or persuade. Their language is generally more informal than in reports, and they use design features to hook the interest of the reader. If you're asked to write a leaflet don't spend too much time on pictures – you can just draw boxes and write in them a few notes about what the picture would show.

A good leaflet will:

- have different types of text (headlines, subheadings, questions, bullet points)
- use short paragraphs
- have a clear sense of audience
- use an appropriate style
- keep the reader's interest throughout.

The next two activities (Tasks 8 and 9) will help you to practise writing leaflets. Task 8 includes an 'Advice' panel to help you. Task 9 has no 'Advice' panel, so you can do this under test conditions.

Task 8

Imagine your school is celebrating its twenty-fifth anniversary and is holding a number of events to mark the occasion. Using the notes on the next page, write a leaflet informing parents about the events and persuading them to become involved. Use the layout format given on the next page. You can add your own words to make the events sound exciting and attractive.

Notes
Thurstington School, Southwold, Suffolk

School play – Bugsy Malone – Thurs/Fri 24/25 June 7.30pm –
a lively and hilarious musical – set in gangland Chicago

Summer concert – string orchestra – jazz band – Year 11 rock
band, 'Haze' – variety of music from the past 250 years – July 11

School activities week – different events for all students –
including canoeing, hiking, Alton Towers, day-trips to local sites,
newspaper – everyone in school will sign up for one or more event

PTA barbecue – parents and staff – school field – Sat July 7

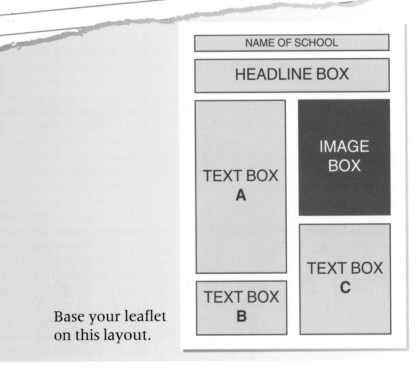

Base your leaflet on this layout.

Advice

The notes provide the information you need. Your task is to make it sound more exciting.

Think of a lively headline.

Think of the image you will use and then write it into the image box.

Remember to use different text styles – for example, questions ('Where were you in 1974?') and bullet points.

Keep the tone light and friendly.

Use a variety of sentences to add interest to your style.

Task 9

Imagine a new youth club is opening in your area. You are part of the committee and want to publicize it. Use the notes below to decide how you will encourage a teenage audience to get involved. Then write your leaflet using the layout design provided.

Notes

Great Framton village hall every Tuesday and Thursday – Tues = 11–14 night; Thurs = 14–16 night

Soft drinks, tea and coffee – darts – table tennis – pool table

Also trips – eg to AquaWorld, shopping in Cambridge

Committee = Richard Corry, Rachel Sunley, David Greenwood, Claire Bradbrook, Peter Worthington – please give any new ideas to them

Come and join committee meetings on first Monday of each month – plan month's activities – look at finances

Plans – trip to theatre in London – Christmas party

Pay each time at door = 50p or term's membership = £4

More details: 01352-7224-53

You can add your own words to make these details sound more exciting. Use the layout provided.

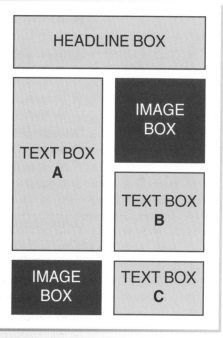

Glossary

active and passive – two ways of using verbs.

    Active: *The Government yesterday announced that…*

    Passive: *It was announced yesterday that…*

Notice how the passive voice disguises the subject – unless we add, 'by the government', we don't know who does the announcing.

adjective – a word which gives more information about a noun or pronoun – e.g. the *white* van; we are *unhappy*.

adverb – a word which gives more information about a verb – such as manner (e.g. *quickly*), time (e.g. *now*) and place (e.g. *here*).

alliteration – the repetition of the same consonant sounds at the start of words in a group, e.g.

    Silently the snow settles.

apostrophe – a punctuation mark used to clarify two types of meaning.

1 It shows when two words have been compressed (is + not = *isn't*). We use this type of expression more in informal situations.

2 It shows that something belongs to someone (*Sam's* feet).

auxiliary verb – a verb which is attached to another verb, in order to show tense, e.g. we *had* arrived early – *had* is the auxiliary verb.

base form – see **root**.

clause – a group of words formed around a verb. They are used to make up sentences. For example, this compound sentence contains two clauses linked by *but*:

    The rain was cold but I enjoyed being there.

Complex sentences are made up of two different types of clause: a **main clause**, and one or more **subordinate clauses**, e.g.

    He swam for half an hour [main clause], *although the water was icy* [subordinate clause].

compressed verb form – a verb (usually a negative) which has been shortened by the addition of an apostrophe, e.g. is + not = *isn't*. See **Apostrophe**.

conjunction – a word used for joining sentences and ideas together. The most commonly-used examples are *and, but, or, because*.

demonstrative adverb – tells us where an action took place, e.g.

> I was happy *there*.

Also known as **adverb of place**.

demonstrative pronoun – tells us whether something is nearby or further away, e.g.

> Look at *this*, not *that*.

determiner – a word which tells us about the noun – for example, *the* cat, *my* cat, *her* cat, *this* cat.

dialect – a regional variety of English. A word like *ginnel* might be used around Leeds, whereas in standard English we would use the word *passageway*.

dialogue – speech between two or more people. (The speech of just one person is known as a **monologue**.)

direct speech – speech which is written down exactly as it was spoken, using speech marks, e.g.

> *He said, 'I can guess what Michael is thinking.'*

The **indirect** or **reported** version of this would be:

> *He said that he could guess what Michael was thinking.*

discourse markers – words which help to make links within texts. They are also called **connectives** or **cohesive devices**. They might include pronouns, e.g. *it, she*, or phrases like *after this, on the other hand*, or adverbs like *therefore, however*. All of these help the reader to follow the thread of a story or argument.

discourse structure – the shape of whole texts: the way they are organized into sections and paragraphs, and how these sections are linked together.

elision – dropping one or more letters from a string of words, usually to reflect the way we say them when we are speaking informally. The elided form of *I do not* is *I don't*. The missing letter has been replaced by an apostrophe.

figurative language – language which includes literary devices, such as similes, metaphors, and personification. Figurative language often uses adjectives and adverbs heavily, too.

fillers – a feature of everyday spoken English. When we speak we use words and phrases like *you know, kind of, er, all right*, often without really noticing that we're using them. They are known as fillers.

imperative – the 'commanding' form of a verb, e.g.

Go away! *Don't* go in there.

Also used in instructions, e.g.

Bake for twenty-five minutes.

An **imperative sentence** is one which begins with an imperative verb, and which gives a command or an instruction.

inflection – to inflect a noun or verb is to change it slightly in order to give it a slightly different meaning. We inflect nouns when we change them from singular to plural, e.g. cat, cat*s*; child, child*ren*.

We inflect verbs when we change their tenses, e.g. we *walk*, we *walked*, we *will walk*.

loan word – a word which has been borrowed from another language. Many loan words in the English language have come from Latin or French, though loan words are also borrowed from other languages, e.g. *piano* (Italian), *pyjamas* (Urdu).

metaphor – a phrase which compares one object to another, to show the reader what it is like, but without using the words *like* or *as*, e.g.

The sea was a monster that night.

See also **Simile**.

noun – a word which labels a person, thing or idea. There are four main types of noun:

common: *hat, chocolate*

proper: *Tony, Tiddles, Taiwan*

abstract: *hatred, unhappiness*

collective: *pack* of cards

Concrete nouns are the same as common nouns: they name physical ('concrete') objects, as opposed to ideas (e.g. *goodness*) or feelings (e.g. *anger*).

object – the object is the person who receives the action of the subject in a sentence. (In 'Fran laughed at Tom' Tom is the object – the person who is being laughed at.)

paragraph – a group of sentences linked together by their theme or topic.

participle – this is the part of the verb that is often found in a phrase, e.g.

Looking in the window, he saw the signs of a fight.

A participle is not strong enough to stand on its own, so in a grammatical sentence it has to be linked to a main verb – in this example, *saw*.

passive voice – see **Active and passive**.

person – this is how we describe the form of the verb used in a sentence: first person (*I*), second person (*you*) and third person (*he* or *she*).

    First person: *I* will always remember the day I left home …
    Second person: *You* always remember the day you left home …
    Third person: *She* would always remember the day she left home …

personification – a technique used by writers to make an abstract concept or an object seem more real and active by giving it human or animal qualities, e.g.

    The wind tapped impatiently at the door.
    Death stalked the battlefields.

phatic phrases – some language is used to keep relationships going. Words and phrases like 'Hello', 'Hi', 'Goodbye', 'Morning' show that we are being polite, rather than serving any important function. They are known as phatic expressions.

phrase – a group of words which makes sense within a clause or sentence but cannot stand on its own – e.g. *on the bus*; *jumping quickly*; *old house*. The last example is a noun phrase – one of the most common types of phrase, in which additional words are grouped around the noun to tell us more about the noun.

plural – more than one.

prefix – letters added in front of the root of a word to change its meaning (e.g. *dis*+like).

preposition – a word used chiefly to show where something or someone is – for example, *in, on, under*.

pronoun – a word which can be used in place of a noun – e.g. *it, her, him, they, we, us*.

relative clauses – clauses that you can add to sentences to give more detail. They begin with *which, who* or *that* – for example:

    My mother, *who is 42 today...*

Relative clauses are also known as **wh- clauses**.

reported speech – also known as **indirect speech**. Reported speech does not use speech marks and usually begins, *He/She said that…*, e.g.

    He said that he could guess what Michael was thinking.

The **direct** version of this would be:

    He said, 'I can guess what Michael is thinking.'

root – the main part of a word without prefixes and suffixes. For example, in *disgracefully* the root is *grace*. The root is also sometimes called the **base form**.

sentence – a group of words which can stand on their own. We expect sentences to:
- contain a main verb
- begin with a capital letter
- end with a full stop, question mark or exclamation mark.

There are three main types of sentence: simple, compound and complex.

A **simple** sentence is made up of one main clause, e.g.
> *The cat sat down.*

A **compound** sentence is made up of two or more main clauses, linked with conjunctions, e.g.
> *The cat sat down and scratched itself.*

A **complex** sentence is made up of a main clause plus one or more subordinate clauses, e.g.
> *The cat scratched itself, as if it had flees.*

simile – a technique used to make writing more visual and interesting. In using similes we use the prepositions *like* or *as* to compare one thing with another, e.g.
> *The wind moved through the woods like a tiger.*

(The wind is being compared to a tiger.)

singular – a word applied to nouns to show that there is only one of them – e.g. *desk, computer, telephone*. These are all singular. To become plural, each would gain an *s*. Some words are the same in their singular and plural forms – e.g. one *sheep*; twenty *sheep*.

standard English – the most important dialect or variety of English. It is used in most written texts, in education, in law, in the media. It is the form of English defined in dictionaries.

subject – the person or thing in a sentence that is doing the action of the verb. (In 'Fran laughed at Tom' Fran is the subject – she is doing the laughing.)

suffix – letters added after the root of a word to change its meaning – e.g. hope + *less*.

syllable – a 'beat' in a word, similar to a beat in music. The word *dog* has just one syllable, while the word *elephant* has three (el-e-phant).

synonym – a word with a similar meaning to another word, e.g. *large* and *big*.

tense – the form of a verb which describes when something happens.

topic sentence – a sentence which summarizes the whole of a newspaper story; usually the first sentence in a news article.

unit of meaning – a part of a word which has its own meaning, e.g. *bi* (means 'two') + *cycle* (means 'wheels') – so the word *bicycle* is made up of two units of meaning.

verb – a word which tells us what someone or something is doing, e.g.
     She *saw* the car. It *slowed* to a standstill.
See also **Auxiliary verb; Compressed verb forms**.

word class – a group of words with a particular function in a sentence – nouns, verbs, adjectives, adverbs, prepositions, conjunctions, and so on. Sometimes called **Parts of speech**.

Acknowledgements

The author and publisher are grateful to the following for permission to reprint copyright material:

Sebastien Berger for extract from article published in the *Daily Telegraph*, 28.5.98, 'Teenager Owen Scores a Record'; **Ian Dicks** for illustrations in The Flora Project for Heart Disease Prevention 'Smoking' leaflet; **Christina Dodwell** for extract from *A Traveller on Horseback* (Hodder & Stoughton, 1987); **Faber & Faber Ltd** for extract from Ted Hughes: *The Iron Man* (Faber, 1968) and for extract from Alan Bennett: *The Lady in the Van* (Faber, 1994); **The Flora Project for Heart Disease Prevention** for text extract from 'Smoking' leaflet; **Diarmid Gunn** on behalf of the Neil Gunn Literary Estate for extract from Neil M Gunn: 'The Tax-Gatherer' in Ian Murray (ed): *The New Penguin Book of Scottish Short Stories* (1983); **David Higham Associates** for extract from Ronald Blythe: *Akenfield* (Penguin, 1969), Copyright © Ronald Blythe 1969; **Hodder and Stoughton Limited** for extract from Keith Waterhouse: 'Shelf-room for Reading' in *Sharon and Tracy and the Rest* (Hodder & Stoughton, 1992); **Mrs J R Kemp** for extract from the War Diary of Sergeant L D Pexton (Imperial War Museum, London); **Macmillan Publishers** for extract from the *Macmillan Encyclopedia* (1987 edition), and extract from Richard Rayner: *The Blue Suit* (Picador, 1995); **Ewan MacNaughton Associates** on behalf of the Telegraph Group Limited for extract from article from the *Daily Telegraph*: 'M1 police clear 20-mile path for runaway lorry' by Barbie Dutter, 11.5.98, Copyright © Telegraph Group Limited, London, 1998; **Mirror Syndication International** for extract from article from *Daily Mirror*, 18.7.97: 'Mind Your Slanguage' by Jo Butler; **National Children's Safety Books** for extracts from Fire Alert leaflet issued by Norfolk and Norwich Hospital; **Penguin Books Ltd** for recipe from Nigel Slater: *The Thirty Minute Cook* (Michael Joseph, 1994), Copyright © Nigel Slater 1994; **The Peters Fraser & Dunlop Group Ltd** for extract from Laurie Lee: *Cider With Rosie* (Penguin, 1962), and extract from Redmond O'Hanlon: *Into the Heart of Borneo* (Penguin, 1985); **Laurence Pollinger Limited** and the Estate of Frieda Lawrence Ravagli for extract from D H Lawrence: 'A Prelude' in *The Mortal Coil and Other Stories* (Penguin, 1971); **The RADIO Magazine** for article by Susan Stranks 23.8.97; **Rogers Coleridge & White** for extract from Kevin Crossley-Holland: 'Mossycoat', Copyright © 1987 Kevin Crossley-Holland, first published in *British Folk Tales* (Orchard Books, 1987); **The Rough Guides** for extract from Alison Gostling: 'Hitching to Lhasa' in Miranda Davies and Natania Jansz (eds): *Women Travel* (Rough Guides, 1990); **Earl Spencer** for extract from his funeral speech for Diana, Princess of Wales; and **Tesco Stores Ltd** for extract from *Tesco Healthy Eating Guide*.

Although every effort has been made to trace and contact copyright holders before publication, this has not always been possible. If notified, the publisher will be pleased to rectify any errors or omissions at the earliest opportunity.

The publishers would like to thank the following for permission to reproduce the following photographs:

Corel: 74
Faber and Faber: 68/Nigel Parry
Hulton Getty 53, 71
Robert Harding Picture Library: 81/R. McLeod, 85/Adam Woolfitt, 116/Ken Gillham
Image Bank: 34/Rita Maas, 45/Tomek Sikora, 62/Todd Davidson, 64/Ian Royd
Lifefile: 76/Richard Powers
Natural History Photographic Library: 21 and 36/David Woodfall, 78/Bill Paton
Popperfoto: 51, 57/Reuters/Monte Fresco
PA News: 93/John Stillwell
Photonica Europe Ltd: cover
Rex Features: 59
Tony Stone: 114/ P. and G. Bowater, 117/Beryl Bidwell
Telegraph Colour Library: 25, 41, 107/Robert Clare
UPI/Corbis – Bettmann: 91